# UK Ninja Dual Zone
# Air Fryer Cookbook

**The Ultimate Guide to Prepare Effortless and Healthy Recipes for Mastering Your Ninja Dual Basket |Full-Colour Edition Incl. FlexDrawer**

*Nancy J. Bryant*

# Copyright© 2024 By Nancy J. Bryant
# All Rights Reserved

This book is copyright protected. It is only for personal use.
You cannot amend, distribute, sell, use,
quote or paraphrase any part of the content within this book,
without the consent of the author or publisher.
Under no circumstances will any blame or
legal responsibility be held against the publisher,
or author, for any damages, reparation,
or monetary loss due to the information contained within this book,
either directly or indirectly.

## Disclaimer Notice:

Please note the information contained within this
document is for educational and entertainment purposes only.
All effort has been executed to present accurate,
up to date, reliable, complete information.
No warranties of any kind are declared or implied.
Readers acknowledge that the author is not engaged
in the rendering of legal,
financial, medical or professional advice.
The content within this book has been derived from various sources.
Please consult a licensed professional before attempting any
techniques outlined in this book.
By reading this document,
the reader agrees that under no circumstances is the
author responsible for any losses,
direct or indirect,
that are incurred as a result of the use of the
information contained within this document, including,
but not limited to, errors, omissions, or inaccuracies.

# Contents

Introduction .................................................. 1

## Chapter 1: Breakfast Recipes .......... 6
Breakfast Filo Tarts ................................. 7
Chipolata Roll-Ups ................................. 7
Baked Avocado Eggs ............................. 8
Cheesy Beans on Toast Twists ............... 8
Protein Flapjacks ................................... 9
Roasted Potatoes with Eggs ................. 9
Spicy Hash Browns .............................. 10
Chocolate Granola .............................. 10
Chinese Dumplings .............................. 11
Chicory Polenta Tart with Sausage ...... 11
Star Anise Muffins ............................... 12
Traditional English Breakfast .............. 12
Grandma's Breakfast Casserole .......... 13
Smoked Salmon Bagel Toasts ............. 13
Easy Breakfast Crumpets .................... 14
Simple Breakfast Wraps ...................... 14

## Chapter 2: Main Recipes ................ 15
Pork and Green Bean Casserole ......... 16
BBQ Duck Wings ................................. 16
Mexican-Style Chicken Meatloaf ........ 17
Moroccan Turkey Salad ...................... 17
Crispy Chicken Bites ........................... 18
Turkey and Quinoa Pilaf ..................... 18
Herb-Roasted Turkey Breast .............. 19
Turkey and Quinoa Bake .................... 19
Easy Pork Burritos .............................. 20
Spicy Roasted Chickpeas .................... 20
Spicy Meatloaves ................................ 21

Sausage and Veggie Traybake ............ 21
Chicken Tikka Masala ......................... 22
Steak and Aubergine Salad ................ 22
Chicken Enchiladas ............................ 23

## Chapter 3: Fish and Seafood ........... 24
Salmon with Capers ........................... 25
Parmesan Crusted Tuna ..................... 25
Sea Scallops ....................................... 26
Aromatic Garlic Cod ........................... 26
Halibut Parcels ................................... 27
Fish and Mushroom Patties ................ 27
King Prawns with Green Beans .......... 28
Cod Fish Croquettes ........................... 28
Fisherman's Tiger Prawns ................... 29
Pesto and Olive Crusted Haddock ...... 29
Stuffed Tomatoes with Tuna .............. 30
Cajun Garlic Butter Shrimp ................. 30
Shrimp Scampi with Linguine ............. 31
Spiced Sea Bass Parcels ..................... 31

## Chapter 4: Poultry and Meat Recipes 32
Mozzarella-Stuffed Pork Medallions ... 33
Chicken with Gnocchi ......................... 33
Beef Pot Roast .................................... 34
Rosemary and Garlic Air-Fried Lamb Chops 34
Rotisserie-Style Roast Chicken ........... 35
Paprika Pork Medallions ..................... 35
Thai Basil Chicken .............................. 36
Korean BBQ Beef Short Ribs .............. 36
Brazilian Picanha Steak ...................... 37
Chinese Honey Sesame Chicken ........ 37

Breaded Veal Cutlets ........................... 38
Mediterranean Poultry Salad ................. 38
Mediterranean Herb Chicken Pasta Bake ... 39
Rosemary Garlic Air Fryer Lamb Steaks ... 39
Beef Sandwiches.................................. 40
BBQ Pulled Pork Loaded Potato Skins ...... 40

## Chapter 5: Healthy Vegetables and Sides
................ 41
Parmesan Roast Asparagus ..................... 42
Cheesy Cauliflower Bites with Yoghurt Dip  42
Curry-Spiced Squash Rings .................. 43
Crispy Brussels Sprouts with Maple Glaze  43
Crispy Kale Chips with Smoked Paprika ... 44
Glazed Root Vegetables ....................... 44
Vegan Air Fryer Falafel ....................... 45
Butternut Squash Wedges ..................... 45
Turmeric-Roasted Chickpeas ................. 46
Grilled Portobello Mushrooms ............... 46
Warm Herbed Cannellini Bean Salad ......... 47
Sesame Soy Broccoli ........................... 47
Spicy Okra ....................................... 48
Baked Potatoes ................................. 48
Crab-Stuffed Mushrooms ...................... 49
Candied Yams with Marshmallows and Pecans
................................................... 49
Tandoori Vegetable Skewers .................. 50

## Chapter 6: Appetisers ........................ 51
Mini Pizza Rolls ................................ 52
Garlic Herb Croutons .......................... 52
Sausage Patty Sliders ......................... 53
Potato Pancakes with Spicy Dip .............. 53

Sticky Spicy Meatballs ........................ 54
Brussels Sprouts with Soy-Maple Glaze...... 54
Falafel with Vegetables ....................... 55
Maple-Glazed Crispy Wings ................... 55
Hummus with Veggie Chips ................... 56
Classic Pesto Sauce............................. 56
Sun-Dried Tomato Tapenade .................. 57
Refried Bean Dip ............................... 57

## Chapter 7: Snacks and Desserts ......... 58
Banana Cupcakes ............................... 59
Easy Almond Fudge ............................ 59
Mini Cherry Bakewell Tarts ................... 60
Classic Brownie ................................ 60
Cinnamon Sugar Apple Chips.................. 61
Cinnamon Apple Fritters....................... 61
Twisted Halloumi Pigs in Blankets............ 62
Peanut Butter Cookies.......................... 62
Mini Autumn Pies .............................. 63
Classic Mug Cake ............................... 63
Mini Sticky Toffee Puddings .................. 64
The Best Crème Brûlée Ever .................. 64
Chinese Spring Rolls With Sweet Chilli Sauce 65

## Chapter 8: Family Favourites ............... 66
Traditional Steak and Kidney Pie ............ 67
Sweet & Sour Chicken Balls .................. 67
Sweet Potato Fries with Cinnamon Sugar and
Nutmeg ........................................... 68

## References ........................... 69

## Image References ........................... 70

# Introduction

If you've ever longed for crispy, golden fries, tenderly roasted vegetables, or perfectly baked goods with less fuss and healthier results, you're in the right place. This book is dedicated to exploring the magic of the Ninja Dual Zone Air Fryer—a versatile kitchen marvel that brings a new dimension to home cooking.

In recent years, air fryers have revolutionised the way we approach cooking, offering a healthier alternative to deep frying without sacrificing flavour or texture. The Ninja Dual Zone Air Fryer, with its cutting-edge technology and dual cooking zones, takes this innovation a step further. It allows you to prepare two different dishes simultaneously at separate temperatures, making it an invaluable tool for busy families, meal preppers, and anyone who enjoys effortless yet impressive meals.

This book is designed to help you make the most of this extraordinary appliance. Inside, you'll find a collection of recipes that celebrate the best of British cuisine, reimagined for the air fryer. From classic comfort foods to contemporary favourites, our aim is to inspire you to experiment and explore. Whether you're craving a hearty Shepherd's Pie, crispy Fish and Chips, or sweet treats like Mini Sticky Toffee Puddings, you'll discover that cooking with the Ninja Dual Zone Air Fryer is both simple and rewarding.

British cooking is renowned for its rich traditions and hearty flavours. However, modern kitchens demand versatility and convenience. The Ninja Dual Zone Air Fryer offers just that, combining the speed and efficiency of air frying with the convenience of dual-zone cooking. This book bridges the gap between traditional British recipes and contemporary cooking techniques, ensuring that you can enjoy the best of both worlds.

Each recipe has been crafted with care to highlight the unique features of the Ninja Dual Zone Air Fryer. You'll find step-by-step instructions, practical tips, and expert advice on how to achieve perfect results every time. From the precise temperature control to the ability to cook two dishes at once, we've taken full advantage of this appliance's capabilities to bring you dishes that are not only delicious but also easy to prepare.

We understand that many of you are eager to embrace new cooking methods without abandoning cherished family recipes. This book acknowledges that sentiment by offering familiar dishes with a modern twist. Our recipes are designed to be straightforward, requiring minimal preparation and cooking time, making them ideal for busy weeknights or special occasions. Each recipe also features guidance on how to adapt traditional methods for the air fryer, ensuring that you can cook with confidence and ease.

As you embark on this culinary journey, we encourage you to experiment and have fun. The Ninja Dual Zone Air Fryer opens up a world of possibilities, allowing you to create mouthwatering dishes that are as enjoyable to make as they are to eat. So, preheat your air fryer, gather your ingredients, and let's explore the exciting potential of this remarkable kitchen appliance together.

Here's to delicious, healthier meals made with the convenience of the Ninja Dual Zone Air Fryer. Happy cooking!

## What Is The Ninja Dual Zone Air Fryer?

The Ninja Dual Zone Air Fryer is a state-of-the-art kitchen appliance that represents a significant leap forward in cooking technology. As the name suggests, this air fryer features two separate cooking zones, each equipped with its own temperature and time controls. This innovative design allows you to cook multiple dishes simultaneously, making it an exceptionally versatile tool for any modern kitchen.

At its core, the Ninja Dual Zone Air Fryer utilises advanced air circulation technology to cook food quickly and evenly. Rapidly circulating hot air around the food mimics the effects of deep frying but with much less oil. This results in dishes that are crispy on the outside and tender on the inside, while significantly reducing the fat content compared to traditional frying

methods. The appliance's dual-zone functionality means you can achieve perfect results for different types of food without the need for preheating or batch cooking.

One of the standout features of the Ninja Dual Zone Air Fryer is its ability to cook two separate dishes at the same time, each at its own temperature. This dual-zone capability is particularly useful for preparing complete meals, allowing you to cook a main dish and a side dish simultaneously. For example, you can air fry crispy chicken wings in one zone while roasting vegetables in the other, all within the same cooking session. This not only saves time but also ensures that your meal is ready all at once, with no need for additional pots or pans.

The air fryer comes equipped with a range of programmable settings designed to simplify cooking. From air frying and roasting to baking and reheating, it offers a variety of cooking modes to suit different recipes. Each zone can be set independently, allowing for even more flexibility in meal preparation. The digital controls are user-friendly and intuitive, making it easy to select the desired cooking mode, adjust the temperature, and set the timer.

Additionally, the Ninja Dual Zone Air Fryer features a non-stick, dishwasher-safe basket, which makes cleaning up after meals a breeze. The appliance's compact design fits comfortably on most countertops while still offering ample cooking capacity. Despite its powerful performance, it operates quietly, ensuring a pleasant cooking experience.

For those who enjoy experimenting with new recipes and flavours, the Ninja Dual Zone Air Fryer provides endless possibilities. It's not just about frying; it's about creating healthier versions of your favourite dishes with less hassle and better results. Whether you're preparing a quick snack or a full family dinner, this air fryer is designed to meet your needs with efficiency and ease.

## Why Use An Air Fryer?

Air fryers have become a beloved appliance in modern kitchens, and for good reason. They offer a range of benefits that make them an attractive alternative to traditional cooking methods. Here's why incorporating an air fryer into your kitchen routine can be a game-changer:

**1. Healthier Cooking**

One of the most significant advantages of using an air fryer is its ability to produce healthier meals. Traditional deep frying requires a substantial amount of oil, which increases the calorie and fat content of foods. In contrast, an air fryer uses hot air to cook food, often requiring little to no oil. This method reduces the fat content by up to 75%, allowing you to enjoy crispy, flavorful dishes with fewer calories and less fat. Whether you're cooking vegetables, meats, or snacks, air frying is a healthier option that doesn't compromise on taste or texture.

**2. Crispy Texture with Less Fat**

Air fryers excel at delivering the crispy texture typically associated with deep-fried foods, but with far less oil. The hot air circulates rapidly around the food, creating a crisp exterior while keeping the inside moist and tender. This makes air fryers perfect for preparing items like fries, chicken wings, and spring rolls, which traditionally rely on deep frying to achieve that satisfying crunch. With an air fryer, you get the same crispy results but with a fraction of the fat.

**3. Faster Cooking Times**

Air fryers are designed to cook food quickly and efficiently. The rapid circulation of hot air reduces cooking times compared to conventional ovens. Preheating is usually unnecessary, which further speeds up the process. This makes air fryers ideal for busy individuals and families who need to prepare meals in less time. Whether you're cooking a quick snack or a full meal, an air fryer can get the job done faster, allowing you to enjoy your food sooner.

**4. Versatility and Convenience**

Air fryers are incredibly versatile appliances that can handle a wide variety of cooking tasks. Beyond frying, they can roast, bake, and even reheat food with ease. Many air fryers come with pre-set cooking programs for popular dishes, making it simple to achieve perfect results every time. Their compact size and ease of use mean they don't require much counter space or complicated setup. Additionally, most air fryer baskets are non-stick and dishwasher-safe, making cleanup a breeze.

**5. Reduced Cooking Odours**

Cooking with an air fryer produces significantly less

odour compared to deep frying or grilling. The enclosed cooking chamber helps to contain and minimise smells, making it a great option for those who want to avoid lingering food odours in the kitchen. This feature is particularly beneficial for preparing dishes with strong smells, such as fish or garlic.

### 6. Safer Cooking

Air fryers offer a safer cooking alternative to deep frying. The absence of hot oil reduces the risk of splatters and burns, making it a safer option for home cooks. Many air fryers also come with built-in safety features, such as automatic shut-off and cool-touch exteriors, further enhancing their safety.

### 7. Energy Efficiency

Compared to traditional ovens, air fryers are more energy-efficient. They heat up quickly and cook food faster, using less electricity overall. This efficiency not only helps to reduce your energy bills but also contributes to a more eco-friendly cooking process.

## The Benefits of Air Frying

Air frying has gained widespread acclaim not just for its health benefits, but also for the practical advantages it offers. Here are some compelling reasons why air frying can transform your cooking experience:

### 1. Enhanced Flavour Profiles

Air frying enhances the natural flavours of your ingredients by concentrating them through rapid, even cooking. Unlike traditional methods that can sometimes dilute flavours or result in uneven seasoning, air frying preserves and intensifies the taste of your food. This means you get richer, more robust flavours without the need for excessive amounts of oil or seasoning.

### 2. Improved Texture Consistency

The air fryer's rapid air circulation ensures a uniform cooking process, resulting in consistently cooked food. This technology reduces the chances of undercooked spots or overly dry areas, which can be common in other cooking methods. With air frying, every bite of your dish achieves the same crispy texture and tender interior, providing a more satisfying eating experience.

### 3. Easy Portion Control

Air fryers typically come with adjustable racks and baskets that make it simple to cook just the right amount of food. This is particularly useful for portion control, whether you're preparing a small meal for one or a larger batch for a family gathering. The ability to adjust cooking quantities easily also helps reduce food waste by allowing you to prepare only what you need.

### 4. Less Need for Added Fats and Oils

Unlike traditional cooking methods that often require significant amounts of oil or butter, air frying uses minimal or no added fats. This feature is beneficial for those who are monitoring their fat intake or aiming to reduce their overall caloric consumption. It allows you to enjoy the same comforting textures and flavours of fried foods without the excess fats.

### 5. Reduced Cleanup Time

The design of air fryers minimises mess and simplifies cleaning. Most air fryer baskets and trays are coated with a non-stick material, making them easy to wipe down and dishwasher-safe. Additionally, the enclosed cooking environment helps to contain splatters and spills, reducing the need for extensive post-cooking cleanup.

### 6. Versatile Cooking Options

Air fryers are versatile appliances capable of handling a range of cooking tasks beyond just frying. They can bake, roast, and grill, making them an all-in-one tool for preparing various dishes. This versatility can streamline your cooking process, allowing you to experiment with different recipes and cooking techniques without needing multiple appliances.

### 7. Less Heating Up of the Kitchen

Unlike traditional ovens that can heat up your entire kitchen, air fryers operate in a compact, enclosed space. This localised heating means you won't have to contend with a hot kitchen, especially during warmer months. It also makes air fryers an efficient choice for quick, everyday cooking without adding extra heat to your home.

### 8. Consistent Results

Air fryers offer consistent cooking results due to their precise temperature control and even heat distribution. This reliability means that you can trust the appliance to deliver the same quality and texture every time you use it. Whether you're cooking a favourite recipe or trying something new, you can expect reliable outcomes without the guesswork.

### 9. Simplified Cooking Techniques
The air fryer's intuitive controls and pre-set cooking modes simplify the cooking process. Many models come with pre-programmed settings for common foods, eliminating the need for trial and error. This user-friendly approach allows even novice cooks to achieve great results with minimal effort.

## Minimising Risks When Air Frying
While air fryers offer a range of benefits, it's important to use them safely and effectively to avoid potential risks. Here are some key practices to minimise risks and ensure a smooth cooking experience with your air fryer:

### 1. Follow Manufacturer Instructions
Always begin by reading the manufacturer's manual and guidelines for your specific air fryer model. Each air fryer may have unique features and recommended safety precautions. Adhering to these instructions helps ensure proper use and reduces the risk of malfunctions or accidents.

### 2. Avoid Overcrowding the Basket
To achieve the best results and ensure even cooking, avoid overcrowding the air fryer basket. When the basket is packed too tightly, hot air cannot circulate properly, leading to uneven cooking and potentially undercooked food. Arrange items in a single layer or cook in batches to maintain optimal airflow and cooking efficiency.

### 3. Use Proper Cooking Utensils
When handling the air fryer basket or tray, use utensils that are safe for non-stick surfaces. Avoid metal utensils that can scratch or damage the non-stick coating, which could affect the appliance's performance and longevity. Opt for silicone or wooden utensils to prevent any damage.

### 4. Monitor Cooking Times and Temperatures
Overcooking or burning food can lead to the release of harmful compounds and negatively impact the taste and texture. Monitor cooking times and temperatures carefully to ensure your food is cooked thoroughly but not excessively. Most air fryers come with built-in timers and temperature controls, so make use of these features to manage your cooking process effectively.

### 5. Keep the Air Fryer Clean
Regular cleaning of your air fryer is crucial for both safety and performance. Residue and grease buildup can become a fire hazard and affect the appliance's functionality. Clean the basket, tray, and interior of the air fryer after each use, following the manufacturer's recommendations. Ensure the appliance is completely cooled before cleaning to prevent burns.

### 6. Handle Hot Surfaces with Care
The exterior of the air fryer and the cooking basket can become very hot during use. Use oven mitts or heat-resistant gloves when handling these parts to avoid burns. Ensure the air fryer is placed on a heat-resistant surface and away from any flammable materials.

### 7. Use the Air Fryer on a Stable Surface
Place your air fryer on a flat, stable surface to prevent tipping or accidents. Ensure there is adequate space around the appliance for proper air circulation and to avoid blocking vents. This stability is important for both the appliance's performance and your safety.

### 8. Ensure Proper Ventilation
Air fryers generate heat and produce steam during cooking. Make sure your kitchen is well-ventilated to handle these byproducts. Avoid using the air fryer in enclosed spaces or areas with poor airflow to reduce the risk of overheating and ensure safe operation.

### 9. Be Cautious with Oil and Fat
While air fryers use less oil than traditional frying, it's important to use oil responsibly. Overusing oil or adding too much can cause excessive smoke or even fires. Follow recipe guidelines for oil quantities and avoid adding oil directly to the hot air fryer basket. Instead, use a spray bottle for even distribution if necessary.

### 10. Address Malfunctions Promptly
If you notice any unusual sounds, smells, or performance issues with your air fryer, address them immediately. Unplug the appliance and inspect it for any visible damage or malfunctions. Consult the manufacturer's customer support or a professional technician if needed to ensure safe and proper repair.

## FAQs For Air Fryer Owners
Air fryers are a popular kitchen appliance, but they

come with a range of features and functions that can sometimes lead to questions. Here are the top eight frequently asked questions about air fryers, along with their answers:

1. How does an air fryer work?

An air fryer works by circulating hot air around food to cook it quickly and evenly. The appliance uses a heating element and a powerful fan to create a convection effect, which cooks food with less oil than traditional frying methods. This results in a crispy exterior and a tender interior, mimicking the texture of fried foods but with significantly less fat.

2. Can I use oil in an air fryer?

Yes, you can use oil in an air fryer, but it's generally used in much smaller quantities than in traditional frying. Adding a small amount of oil—either through a spritz or a light brush—can enhance the crispiness and flavour of your food. However, many recipes and foods will cook well without any added oil at all. It's important to avoid adding too much oil, as it can lead to excessive smoke and potential safety hazards.

3. What types of food can I cook in an air fryer?

Air fryers are versatile appliances that can cook a wide variety of foods. You can use them to prepare items like vegetables, meats, poultry, seafood, frozen snacks, and even baked goods. The appliance is capable of frying, roasting, baking, and grilling. For best results, follow specific recipes and adjust cooking times and temperatures according to the type of food you are preparing.

4. How do I clean my air fryer?

Cleaning your air fryer is straightforward but essential for maintaining its performance and safety. After each use, unplug the appliance and allow it to cool completely. Remove the basket and tray, and wash them with warm, soapy water or in the dishwasher if they are dishwasher-safe. Wipe down the interior of the air fryer with a damp cloth or sponge to remove any food particles or grease. Ensure that all components are thoroughly dried before reassembling or storing the appliance.

5. Can I cook frozen food in an air fryer?

Yes, air fryers are excellent for cooking frozen foods. They can quickly cook frozen fries, chicken nuggets, and other pre-packaged items without needing to thaw them first. Adjust the cooking time and temperature as needed, and be sure to shake or stir the food halfway through cooking to ensure even results. Always follow the manufacturer's guidelines for cooking times and temperatures for specific frozen items.

6. How long does it take to preheat an air fryer?

Most air fryers do not require a long preheat time. In fact, many models reach the desired temperature within a few minutes. Some air fryers have a preheat function that automatically heats the appliance before cooking begins. For those that don't, simply set the air fryer to the desired cooking temperature for a few minutes before adding your food. This step ensures that your food starts cooking at the correct temperature, resulting in more consistent and evenly cooked results.

7. Can I use aluminium foil or parchment paper in my air fryer?

Yes, you can use aluminium foil or parchment paper in an air fryer, but it's important to use them correctly. Ensure that any foil or paper is placed in the basket or tray without covering the vents or obstructing the airflow. This prevents interference with the cooking process and ensures that hot air can circulate properly around the food. Use these materials to make cleanup easier or to prevent sticky foods from adhering to the basket.

8. What should I do if my air fryer starts smoking?

If your air fryer starts smoking, it could be due to several reasons, such as excess oil, food residue, or high-fat content in the food being cooked. To address this, immediately stop the cooking process and unplug the appliance. Allow it to cool before checking for any residue or grease buildup. Clean the basket and interior thoroughly, and avoid using too much oil. If smoking persists, ensure that the appliance is not overheating and that it is placed on a stable, heat-resistant surface.

By understanding these frequently asked questions, you can optimise your air fryer use and enjoy all the benefits it offers. If you have any further questions or issues, consulting the user manual or reaching out to the manufacturer's support can provide additional assistance.

# 1
# Breakfast Recipes

# Breakfast Filo Tarts

Serves: 8 / Prep time: 10 minutes / Cook time: 10 minutes

### Ingredients
- Eight sheets of filo pastry (approx. 350g)
- 200g chopped ham
- 100ml tomato sauce
- 200g crumbled mozzarella cheese
- 20g melted butter

### Instructions
1. Preheat your Ninja Dual Zone Air Fryer to 180°C for 5 minutes. Lightly grease 8 muffin cases or line them with baking paper.
2. Let the filo pastry thaw as per the package Instructions. Stack the sheets on a flat surface, then cut them into eight squares and press each square into a muffin case.
3. In a bowl, mix the ham, tomato sauce, and mozzarella. Evenly distribute this mixture among the prepared muffin cases. Place the cases into the air fryer drawers.
4. Set zone 1 to "BAKE" at 180°C for 10 minutes or until the pastry is golden brown. Select "MATCH" and press the "START/STOP" button.
5. Serve warm with your favourite toppings.

# Chipolata Roll-Ups

Serves: 8 / Prep time: 5 minutes / Cook time: 26 minutes

### Ingredients
- Eight chipolatas
- 2 x 250g packs of croissant dough
- 1 tbsp English mustard
- 2 tbsp tomato ketchup
- 1 beaten egg
- 1 tbsp sesame seeds

### Instructions
1. Arrange the chipolatas in both air fryer drawers. Set zone 1 to "AIR FRY" at 200°C for 16 minutes or until golden brown. Select "MATCH" and press the "START/STOP" button.
2. Unroll the croissant dough and place a sausage on the wide end of each dough triangle. Spread mustard and ketchup on the sausage, then roll it up. Place the roll-ups on two baking trays, brush with beaten egg, and sprinkle with sesame seeds.
3. Set zone 1 to "BAKE" at 180°C for 10 minutes or until golden. Select "MATCH" and press the "START/STOP" button.
4. Enjoy hot and fresh!

## Baked Avocado Eggs

Serves: 6 / Prep time: 10 minutes / Cook time: 10 minutes

### Ingredients
- Three large avocados, halved and pitted
- Six small eggs
- Garlic salt and cayenne pepper, to taste
- 100g cooked and crumbled bacon
- 35g crumbled parmesan cheese
- 2 tbsp lemon juice
- 1/2 tsp garlic granules
- 1 tbsp yellow mustard

### Instructions
1. Halve the avocados and carefully remove the pits.
2. Scoop out 1-2 tablespoons of avocado flesh from each half and set aside.
3. Crack an egg into each avocado half. Season with garlic salt and cayenne pepper, then top with crumbled bacon. Place the avocados into both air fryer drawers.
4. Set zone 1 to "BAKE" at 190°C for 10 minutes. Select "MATCH" and press "START/STOP."
5. Midway through cooking, sprinkle parmesan cheese over the avocado eggs. Reinsert the drawers to continue cooking.
6. Meanwhile, mash the reserved avocado with lemon juice, garlic granules, and yellow mustard.
7. Drizzle the sauce over the avocado eggs before serving.

## Cheesy Beans on Toast Twists

Serves: 4 / Prep time: 10 minutes / Cook time: 15 minutes

### Ingredients:
- 400g canned baked beans
- 100g grated cheddar cheese
- Four slices of whole-grain bread
- 2 tbsp melted butter
- 1 tsp dried mixed herbs
- Salt and black pepper, to taste

### Preparation Instructions:
1. Preheat your Ninja Dual Zone Air Fryer to 180°C for 5 minutes.
2. In a bowl, combine the baked beans, grated cheddar, dried herbs, salt, and pepper.
3. Slice the whole-grain bread into smaller portions, or use a cookie cutter for fun shapes.
4. Brush both sides of each piece of bread with melted butter.
5. Place the bread in the air fryer basket and cook at 180°C for 5 minutes or until golden and crispy.
6. Top the toasted bread with the cheesy baked beans mixture.
7. Air fry for an additional 5-8 minutes until the cheese is melted and bubbly.
8. Serve hot and enjoy your Cheesy Beans on Toast Twists!

# Protein Flapjacks

Serves: 8-10 / Prep time: 10 minutes / Cook time: 20 minutes

### Ingredients
- 300g rolled oats
- 100g clear honey (or acacia honey)
- 2 tbsp chia seeds
- 2 tbsp chopped almonds
- 200g peanut butter
- A pinch of sea salt
- A pinch of grated nutmeg
- 1/2 tsp cinnamon powder

### Instructions
1. Preheat your Ninja Dual Zone Air Fryer to 175°C. Lightly grease two baking tins with nonstick spray.
2. In a food processor, combine the oats, honey, chia seeds, almonds, peanut butter, salt, nutmeg, and cinnamon until mixed.
3. Spread the mixture evenly into the prepared tins. Place the tins into the air fryer drawers.
4. Set zone 1 to "BAKE" at 180°C for 20 minutes. Select "MATCH" and press "START/STOP."
5. Allow the flapjacks to cool for about 10 minutes before slicing them into bars or squares.

# Roasted Potatoes with Eggs

Serves: 4 / Prep time: 5 minutes / Cook time: 22 minutes

### Ingredients
- 600g diced yellow potatoes
- 1 tbsp softened butter
- One chopped bell pepper
- One chopped chilli pepper
- Sea salt and black pepper, to taste
- 1 tsp dried rosemary
- 1 tsp garlic granules
- 1 tsp onion powder
- Four medium eggs

### Instructions
1. Mix the diced potatoes with butter, bell pepper, chilli pepper, and spices.
2. Whisk the eggs with salt and pepper, then pour into four silicone muffin cups (or two ramekins).
3. Add the potatoes to zone 1 of the air fryer and the eggs to zone 2.
4. Set zone 1 to "ROAST" at 190°C for 22 minutes and zone 2 to "AIR FRY" at 180°C for 10 minutes.
5. Select "SYNC" and press "START/STOP." Midway through, shake the potatoes to ensure even cooking.

## Spicy Hash Browns

Serves: 6-8 / Prep time: 10 minutes / Cook time: 30 minutes

### Ingredients
- 600g potatoes (such as Maris Piper or King Edward)
- Sea salt and black pepper, to taste
- 1 tsp chilli flakes
- 50g melted butter

### Instructions
1. Boil the potatoes for 15 minutes, then drain and peel them. Grate the potatoes coarsely into a bowl and season with salt, pepper, and chilli flakes.
2. Stir in the melted butter until well combined, then divide the mixture into 6-8 greased muffin cups.
3. Place the muffin cups into both air fryer drawers.
4. Set zone 1 to "AIR FRY" at 200°C for 15 minutes. Select "MATCH" and press "START/STOP."
5. Serve with your favourite tomato sauce.

## Chocolate Granola

Serves: 10-12 / Prep time: 10 minutes / Cook time: 15 minutes

### Ingredients
- 200g rolled oats
- 100g cornflakes
- 100g chopped almonds (or hazelnuts)
- 40g coconut oil
- 50g clear honey
- 50g sunflower seeds
- 80g pumpkin seeds
- 1 tsp ground cinnamon
- A pinch of coarse sea salt
- 100g chopped or shaved chocolate

### Instructions
1. Preheat your Ninja Dual Zone Air Fryer to 180°C. Line two roasting tins with baking paper.
2. Mix the oats, cornflakes, almonds, coconut oil, and 20g of honey. Spread this mixture onto one roasting tin and place it in zone 1 of the air fryer.
3. Combine the seeds with the remaining honey, cinnamon, and salt; spread onto the second tin and place in zone 2.
4. Set zone 1 to "ROAST" at 170°C for 15 minutes and zone 2 to "ROAST" at 160°C for 9 minutes. Select "SYNC" and press "START/STOP."
5. Stir the contents of zone 1 when 7 minutes remain and zone 2 when 4 minutes remain.
6. After cooking, mix the oats and seeds together, then stir in the chocolate while the granola is still warm. Enjoy!

# Chinese Dumplings

Serves: 2 / Prep time: 5 minutes / Cook time: 12 minutes

### Ingredients:
- Dumpling wrappers
- 110g minced beef
- Two chopped scallions
- 1 tsp garlic powder
- 2 tbsp oyster sauce
- Cooking spray

### Preparation Instructions:
1. In a bowl, mix together the minced beef, chopped scallions, garlic powder, and oyster sauce.
2. Place 1 tablespoon of the filling onto each dumpling wrapper.
3. Fold the wrappers and pinch the tops to seal them securely.
4. Lightly spray the dumplings with oil.
5. Set the air fryer to 190°C and cook for 10-12 minutes, flipping the dumplings halfway through. Enjoy!

# Chicory Polenta Tart with Sausage

Serves: 6 / Prep time: 5 minutes / Cook time: 20 minutes

### Ingredients
- 600ml vegetable stock
- 200g instant polenta
- 1 tbsp olive oil
- 4 smoked sausages, sliced
- 180g cheddar cheese, thinly sliced
- Two heads of red chicory, halved
- 1/2 tsp chilli flakes
- Sea salt and ground black pepper, to taste

### Instructions
1. Heat the vegetable stock in a large saucepan until it boils, then reduce the heat to medium-low. Gradually whisk in the polenta and olive oil to avoid lumps.
2. Let the polenta simmer for about 5 minutes, whisking continuously. Once done, pour the polenta into two lightly greased baking trays and allow it to cool.
3. Place the trays in the air fryer drawers.
4. Select zone 1 and set it to "BAKE" at 190°C for 20 minutes. Use the "MATCH" function to apply the same settings to zone 2. Press "START/STOP."
5. Halfway through, add the sausage slices and cheese on top of the polenta, then reinsert the drawers to continue cooking.
6. Garnish the polenta tarts with chicory, chilli flakes, and seasoning before serving warm or at room temperature.

# Star Anise Muffins

Serves: 8 / Prep time: 10 minutes / Cook time: 15 minutes

### Ingredients
- Two large eggs
- 200g brown sugar
- 200g self-raising flour
- 1/4 tsp ground anise
- 1/4 tsp ground cinnamon
- 300g apple sauce
- 100g coconut oil
- A pinch of sea salt

### Preparation Instructions
1. Remove the crisper plate from your Ninja Foodi and preheat it to 160°C for 5 minutes. Lightly grease eight muffin cases with nonstick spray.
2. In a mixing bowl, whisk the eggs until pale and frothy. Gradually add the apple sauce, brown sugar, and coconut oil, stirring until combined.
3. In another bowl, combine the dry Ingredients.
4. Slowly fold the dry mixture into the wet Ingredients until fully incorporated. Spoon the batter into the prepared muffin cases and place 4 cases in each drawer.
5. Set zone 1 to "BAKE" at 160°C for 15 minutes. Select "MATCH" and press "START/STOP."
6. Let the muffins cool on a rack for 10 minutes before serving.

# Traditional English Breakfast

Serves: 5 / Prep time: 10 minutes / Cook time: 16 minutes

### Ingredients
- 250g quartered brown mushrooms
- Two small tomatoes halved
- Sea salt and black pepper, to taste
- 1/2 tsp crushed red pepper flakes
- Five rashers of smoked bacon
- Four breakfast sausage links
- 100g drained canned baked beans

### Preparation Instructions
1. Toss the mushrooms and tomatoes with salt, black pepper, and red pepper flakes. Insert crisper plates into both air fryer drawers and spray with nonstick cooking oil.
2. Place the mushrooms, tomatoes, and bacon in zone 1 and the sausages in zone 2.
3. Set zone 1 to "AIR FRY" at 180°C for 9 minutes and zone 2 to "AIR FRY" at 200°C for 16 minutes.
4. Select "SYNC" and press "START/STOP." Midway through cooking, shake or toss the Ingredients to ensure even cooking.
5. Arrange the cooked Ingredients on plates and serve with baked beans. Optionally, add black pudding and fried eggs for a full English breakfast experience.

# Grandma's Breakfast Casserole

Serves: 6 / Prep time: 10 minutes / Cook time: 15 minutes

## Ingredients
- 300g beef sausage, crumbled
- One medium shallot, thinly sliced
- One green pepper, seeded and diced
- 250g chestnut mushrooms, sliced
- Eight large eggs, beaten
- 100ml whole milk
- 125g cheddar cheese, grated
- Garlic salt and ground black pepper, to taste

## Instructions
1. Combine all the Ingredients in a large mixing bowl, stirring until well mixed.
2. Pour the mixture into two lightly greased baking tins, then place them in the air fryer drawers.
3. Select zone 1 and set it to "BAKE" at 190°C for 15 minutes. Use the "MATCH" function to mirror the settings for zone 2. Press "START/STOP."
4. At the halfway mark, gently stir the mixture. Reinsert the drawers to finish cooking.

# Smoked Salmon Bagel Toasts

Serves: 8 / Prep time: 10 minutes / Cook time: 6 minutes

## Ingredients
- Four whole-grain bagels, split
- 1 tsp olive oil
- 200g cream cheese
- 2 (120g) packs smoked salmon trimmings
- Sea salt and ground black pepper, to taste
- 1 tbsp capers, drained
- One small lemon, sliced

## Instructions
1. Lightly brush both sides of the bagel halves with olive oil.
2. Assemble the bagels by spreading a generous layer of cream cheese on each half, then topping with smoked salmon, salt, pepper, and capers.
3. Place the prepared bagels into both air fryer drawers.
4. Select zone 1 and set it to "BAKE" at 190°C for 6 minutes. Use the "MATCH" function for zone 2. Press "START/STOP."
5. Garnish the bagels with lemon slices and serve immediately while still warm. Enjoy!

# Easy Breakfast Crumpets

Serves: 4 / Prep time: 10 minutes / Cook time: 6 minutes

### Ingredients
- Four large crumpets
- 1 tbsp melted butter
- Four medium eggs
- 100g cheddar cheese, shredded
- 4 (30g) rashers of back bacon
- 4 tbsp passata
- Sea salt and cayenne pepper, to taste

### Instructions
1. Brush the crumpets with melted butter on both sides.
2. Beat the eggs and mix them with the shredded cheese.
3. Prepare the crumpets by spreading passata on each, then topping with the egg mixture and bacon. Place them in the air fryer basket.
4. Select zone 1 and set it to "BAKE" at 190°C for 6 minutes. Use the "MATCH" function to apply the same settings to zone 2. Press "START/STOP."

# Simple Breakfast Wraps

Serves: 5 / Prep time: 10 minutes / Cook time: 21 minutes

### Ingredients
- 400g breakfast sausage, sliced
- 500g button mushrooms, quartered
- 1 tsp olive oil
- Sea salt and ground black pepper, to taste
- 1/2 tsp garlic powder
- Five tortilla wraps
- One pepper, seeded and sliced
- 100g canned chickpeas, drained

### Preparation Instructions
1. Insert a crisper plate in both air fryer drawers and lightly coat them with nonstick spray.
2. Add the breakfast sausage to zone 1.
3. Toss the mushrooms in olive oil, season with salt, pepper, and garlic powder, then place them in zone 2.
4. Set zone 1 to "AIR FRY" at 200°C for 16 minutes and zone 2 to "AIR FRY" at 200°C for 12 minutes.
5. Use the "SYNC" function, then press "START/STOP." At the halfway point, give the food a shake or toss it using silicone-tipped tongs.
6. To assemble the wraps, divide the sausage, mushrooms, bell pepper, and chickpeas among the tortillas and wrap them up.
7. Place the wraps back into the air fryer drawers. Select "REHEAT" at 170°C for 5 minutes. Enjoy your meal!

#  2

# Main Recipes

# Pork and Green Bean Casserole

Serves: 6 / Prep time: 5 minutes / Cook time: 40 minutes

### Ingredients
- 1 tbsp olive oil
- 100g bacon lardons
- 800g ground beef
- 100ml tomato purée
- 100ml hot water
- 1 tbsp beef bouillon granules
- 1 tsp paprika
- One onion, chopped
- One celery stalk, chopped
- One carrot, chopped
- 200g green beans
- 150g Parmesan cheese, freshly grated

### Instructions
1. Mix all Ingredients except for the cheese in a large bowl until thoroughly combined.
2. Spoon the mixture into two greased baking tins and place in the air fryer drawers without crisper plates.
3. Set zone 1 to "ROAST" at 180°C for 40 minutes. Use the "MATCH" function to duplicate settings for zone 2. Press "START/STOP."
4. Halfway through cooking, stir the Ingredients gently and top with Parmesan cheese. Reinsert drawers to finish cooking.

# BBQ Duck Wings

Serves: 4 / Prep time: 5 minutes / Cook time: 25 minutes

### Ingredients
- 1kg duck wings, boneless
- 1 tbsp olive oil
- 1 tbsp maple syrup
- 1 tsp ginger-garlic paste
- 100ml BBQ sauce • Sea salt and ground black pepper, to taste

### Instructions
1. In a large bowl, toss the duck wings with olive oil, maple syrup, ginger-garlic paste, and BBQ sauce.
2. Place the wings into the air fryer basket.
3. Set zone 1 to "AIR FRY" at 195°C for 25 minutes. Use the "MATCH" function to apply the settings to zone 2. Press "START/STOP."
4. When 15 minutes remain, turn the wings over and baste them with the remaining sauce. Reinsert the drawers to finish cooking. Enjoy!

# Mexican-Style Chicken Meatloaf

Serves: 8 / Prep time: 10 minutes / Cook time: 20 minutes

### Ingredients
- 1kg chicken breast, chopped
- One garlic clove, minced
- One medium onion, chopped
- One jalapeño pepper, seeded and minced
- One celery stalk, chopped
- Two medium peppers, halved and seeded
- 1 tbsp taco seasoning
- 100g sharp cheese, grated
- Sea salt and ground black pepper, to taste
- One medium egg, beaten
- 50ml buttermilk

### Instructions
1. Lightly grease two loaf tins with nonstick spray.
2. In a mixing bowl, thoroughly combine all the Ingredients. Pour the mixture into the prepared loaf tins.
3. Spray the tops of the meatloaves with cooking oil. Place a loaf tin in each air fryer drawer.
4. Set zone 1 to "AIR FRY" at 180°C for 20 minutes. Use the "MATCH" function to mirror the settings for zone 2. Press "START/STOP."
5. Allow the meatloaves to rest for about 10 minutes before slicing and serving. Enjoy!

# Moroccan Turkey Salad

Serves: 5 / Prep time: 10 minutes / Cook time: 50 minutes

### Ingredients
- 600g turkey breast, skinless and boneless
- One medium aubergine, peeled and sliced
- 1 tsp cayenne pepper
- 1 tsp mustard powder
- Sea salt and ground black pepper, to taste
- 2 tbsp extra-virgin olive oil
- Two spring onions, sliced
- One large tomato, diced
- One small cucumber, peeled and diced
- One small head of lettuce

### Instructions
1. Place the turkey and aubergine slices in a resealable bag along with the spices and olive oil; shake until well coated.
2. Place the turkey in zone 1 and the aubergine in zone 2.
3. Set zone 1 to "AIR FRY" at 180°C for 50 minutes and zone 2 to "ROAST" at 200°C for 8 minutes. Use the "SYNC" function and press "START/STOP."
4. Turn the turkey and aubergine halfway through cooking to ensure even browning.
5. Slice the cooked turkey into strips and add them to a salad bowl with the roasted aubergine and remaining salad Ingredients. Toss gently to combine. Enjoy!

# Crispy Chicken Bites

Serves: 4 / Prep time: 10 minutes + marinating time / Cook time: 18 minutes

### Ingredients
- 600g chicken breast, diced into small chunks
- 100ml plain yoghurt
- Sea salt and freshly ground black pepper, to taste
- 1 tsp paprika
- 100g crushed cornflakes
- 1 tbsp olive oil

### Instructions
1. Combine the chicken pieces with yoghurt, salt, pepper, and paprika in a ceramic bowl. Let it marinate in the refrigerator for about 3 hours.
2. Discard the marinade and coat each chicken piece in the crushed cornflakes, pressing gently to adhere. Brush with olive oil and arrange in the air fryer basket.
3. Set zone 1 to "AIR FRY" at 200°C for 18 minutes. Use the "MATCH" function to mirror the settings for zone 2. Press "START/STOP."
4. Halfway through cooking, shake the basket for even cooking. Return the drawers and finish cooking. Enjoy!

# Turkey and Quinoa Pilaf

Serves: 4 / Prep time: 10 minutes / Cook time: 35 minutes

### Ingredients
- 600g turkey breast, boneless and skinless, chopped
- 2 tbsp olive oil
- 1 tsp poultry seasoning
- One onion, finely chopped
- Two garlic cloves, minced
- 1 (400g) can of diced tomatoes
- 600ml hot chicken broth
- 200g quinoa, rinsed

### Instructions
1. Toss the turkey with olive oil and poultry seasoning. Mix in the remaining Ingredients.
2. Divide the mixture between two baking trays, cover with foil, and place in the air fryer drawers.
3. Set zone 1 to "AIR FRY" at 190°C for 35 minutes. Use the "MATCH" function to sync both zones. Press "START/STOP."
4. At the halfway mark, remove the foil and continue cooking.
5. Serve warm and enjoy!

# Herb-Roasted Turkey Breast

Serves: 4 / Prep time: 5 minutes / Cook time: 1 hour

**Ingredients**
- 1kg turkey breast, boneless with skin, halved
- 30g softened butter
- One bay leaf
- One sprig of rosemary, finely chopped
- Two garlic cloves, minced
- 1 tbsp English mustard
- Sea salt and freshly ground black pepper, to taste

**Instructions**
1. Insert crisper plates into both air fryer drawers and spray with nonstick cooking oil.
2. Pat turkey breasts dry with a paper towel. Use a mortar and pestle to crush the garlic, rosemary, and bay leaf.
3. Rub the turkey thoroughly with the butter and spice mixture, then place the breasts onto the prepared crisper plates.
4. Select zone 1 and set it to "ROAST" at 200°C for 1 hour. Use the "MATCH" function to duplicate the settings for zone 2. Press "START/STOP."
5. Turn the turkey breasts over halfway through to ensure even cooking. Reinsert drawers and finish cooking.

# Turkey and Quinoa Bake

Serves: 6 / Prep time: 10 minutes / Cook time: 35 minutes

**Ingredients**
- 500g ground turkey
- 1 tsp poultry seasoning
- 100g pancetta, diced
- 1 tbsp olive oil
- One onion, chopped
- Two garlic cloves, minced
- One pepper, deseeded and sliced
- 1 (400g) can of diced tomatoes
- 600ml hot chicken broth
- 200g quinoa, rinsed

**Instructions**
1. Combine the ground turkey with poultry seasoning. Stir in the other Ingredients.
2. Divide the mixture between two baking trays, cover with foil, and place in the air fryer drawers.
3. Set zone 1 to "AIR FRY" at 190°C for 35 minutes. Use the "MATCH" function to sync both zones. Press "START/STOP."
4. Remove the foil halfway through cooking and return the drawers to finish.

# Easy Pork Burritos

Serves: 5 / Prep time: 10 minutes / Cook time: 55 minutes

### Ingredients
- 1kg pork shoulder, cut into four pieces
- 1 tbsp olive oil
- 1 tsp mustard powder
- 1 tsp garlic granules
- 1 tsp onion powder
- Sea salt and freshly ground black pepper, to taste
- 3 tbsp tomato paste
- 100ml chicken broth
- One jalapeño pepper, seeded and minced
- Five medium tortillas
- 500g cooked rice
- 200g black beans, drained and rinsed

### Instructions
1. Insert crisper plates in both air fryer drawers and spray with nonstick cooking oil.
2. Toss the pork shoulder pieces with olive oil and spices. Divide the pork between the drawers.
3. Select zone 1 and set it to "ROAST" at 175°C for 55 minutes. Use the "MATCH" function to mirror the settings for zone 2. Press "START/STOP."
4. Turn the pork pieces halfway through cooking and reinsert the drawers.
5. Shred the cooked pork and distribute it between tortillas along with the rice, beans, and jalapeño. Roll up the burritos.
6. Place the burritos in the drawers and set zone 1 to "REHEAT" at 160°C for 5 minutes. Enjoy!

# Spicy Roasted Chickpeas

Serves: 4-5 / Prep time: 10 minutes / Cook time: 13 minutes

### Ingredients
- 2 (400g) cans chickpeas, drained and rinsed
- 1 tbsp olive oil
- 1 tsp ground cumin
- 1 tsp chilli powder
- Sea salt and freshly ground black pepper, to taste

### Instructions
1. Toss the chickpeas in olive oil and season with cumin, chilli powder, salt, and pepper.
2. Divide the chickpeas between zones 1 and 2 of the air fryer.
3. Set zone 1 to "ROAST" at 190°C for 13 minutes. Use the "MATCH" function to duplicate settings for zone 2. Press "START/STOP."
4. Shake the baskets halfway through cooking for even browning. Enjoy!

# Spicy Meatloaves

Serves: 6 / Prep time: 10 minutes / Cook time: 25 minutes

### Ingredients
- 300g ground pork
- 300g ground beef
- 100g bacon lardons
- 50g fresh breadcrumbs
- 50g parmesan cheese, grated
- One pepper, deseeded and chopped
- One onion, finely chopped
- Two garlic cloves, minced
- Sea salt and freshly ground black pepper, to taste

### Instructions
1. Grease two loaf tins with nonstick cooking spray. In a small bowl, mix 25g of breadcrumbs with 25g of parmesan and set aside.
2. Combine the remaining Ingredients thoroughly and press into the prepared loaf tins. Sprinkle the reserved breadcrumb and parmesan mixture on top.
3. Spray the tops with cooking oil. Place a loaf tin in each air fryer drawer.
4. Set zone 1 to "AIR FRY" at 180°C for 25 minutes. Use the "MATCH" function to mirror settings across both zones. Press "START/STOP."
5. Allow the meatloaves to rest for about 10 minutes before slicing and serving.

# Sausage and Veggie Traybake

Serves: 4 / Prep time: 10 minutes / Cook time: 15 minutes

### Ingredients
- 600g pork sausages, casings removed, cut into chunks
- Two medium carrots, cut into 1.5cm pieces
- One celery stalk, sliced into 1.5cm pieces
- Two small onions, quartered
- 1 tbsp olive oil
- 1/2 tsp hot paprika
- 1 tsp garlic granules
- 1 tsp mustard powder
- Sea salt and freshly ground black pepper, to taste

### Instructions
1. Toss the vegetables in olive oil and season with spices until evenly coated.
2. Place the sausage pieces in the zone 1 drawer using a lightly greased crisper plate.
3. Arrange the vegetables in a lightly greased roasting tin and place them in the zone 2 drawer.
4. Set zone 1 to "AIR FRY" at 200°C for 15 minutes and zone 2 to "ROAST" at 190°C for 13 minutes. Use the "SYNC" function and press "START/STOP."
5. Halfway through, turn the sausages and stir the vegetables, then return to the drawers to continue cooking.
6. Serve the sausages and vegetables together from the tray.

# Chicken Tikka Masala

Serves: 4 / Prep time: 30 minutes (+1 hour marinating time) / Cook time: 15 minutes

### Ingredients
- 500g boneless, skinless chicken breasts, cubed
- 200g plain yoghurt
- 3 tbsp tomato paste
- 2 cloves garlic, minced
- 2 tsp ground cumin
- 2 tsp ground coriander
- 2 tsp paprika
- 1 tsp ground turmeric
- 1 tsp garam masala
- 1/2 tsp chilli powder (adjust to taste)
- 1 tbsp vegetable oil
- Salt, to taste
- Fresh cilantro for garnish

### Instructions
1. Combine the yoghurt, tomato paste, garlic, cumin, coriander, paprika, turmeric, garam masala, chilli powder, vegetable oil, and salt in a bowl to create the marinade.
2. Add the chicken to the marinade, ensuring it's evenly coated. Cover and refrigerate for at least 1 hour.
3. Preheat the Ninja Dual Zone Air Fryer to 200°C in zone 1 for 5 minutes.
4. Place the marinated chicken in zone 1 and cook at 200°C for 12-15 minutes, turning halfway, until cooked through and slightly charred.
5. Let the chicken rest for a few minutes before serving. Garnish with fresh cilantro and serve with steamed rice and naan.

# Steak and Aubergine Salad

Serves: 4 / Prep time: 10 minutes / Cook time: 20 minutes

### Ingredients
- 500g skirt steak, thinly sliced
- 500g aubergine, sliced
- 2 tbsp extra-virgin olive oil
- Two garlic cloves, minced
- Sea salt and freshly ground black pepper, to taste
- One large tomato, diced
- One small cucumber, sliced
- One medium onion, thinly sliced
- 2 tbsp fresh lemon juice

### Instructions
1. Toss the steak and aubergine with one tablespoon of olive oil, minced garlic, salt, and pepper.
2. Place the steak in the zone 1 drawer and the aubergine slices in the zone 2 drawer.
3. Set zone 1 to "AIR FRY" at 195°C for 20 minutes and zone 2 to "ROAST" at 200°C for 8 minutes. Use the "SYNC" function and press "START/STOP."
4. Turn the Ingredients halfway through for even cooking. Reinsert drawers and continue cooking.
5. Slice the steak into strips and combine with the aubergine, tomato, cucumber, onion, and lemon juice in a salad bowl. Toss to mix.

# Chicken Enchiladas

Serves: 4 / Prep time: 10 minutes / Cook time: 1 hour

### Ingredients
- 800g boneless, skinless chicken cut into small pieces
- Sea salt and ground black pepper, to taste
- 1 tsp olive oil
- Eight small tortillas
- 100g grated cheese
- For the Enchilada Sauce:
- 1 tbsp olive oil
- 1 tsp garlic powder
- 100ml tomato paste
- 100ml chicken broth
- One jalapeño pepper, seeded and minced

### Instructions
1. Insert crisper plates into both air fryer drawers and lightly coat them with nonstick spray.
2. Season the chicken with salt, pepper, and olive oil, then divide the pieces between the drawers.
3. Set zone 1 to "ROAST" at 170°C for 45 minutes. Use the "MATCH" function to duplicate the settings for zone 2. Press "START/STOP."
4. At the halfway point, turn the chicken pieces to ensure even cooking, then reinsert the drawers.
5. While the chicken is cooking, prepare the enchilada sauce by mixing all the sauce Ingredients together.
6. Once the chicken is done, divide it among the tortillas, top with half the grated cheese, and roll them up to form enchiladas.
7. Place the enchiladas into two lightly greased baking tins, cover with sauce, sprinkle with the remaining cheese, and place the tins in the air fryer drawers (without crisper plates).
8. Set zone 1 to "BAKE" at 190°C for 15 minutes until the tops are golden brown. Use the "MATCH" function to apply the settings to zone 2. Press "START/STOP." Enjoy your meal!

# 3
# Fish and Seafood

## Salmon with Capers

Serves: 4 / Prep time: 10 minutes / Cook time: 12 minutes

**Ingredients:**
- 800g salmon fillets
- 1 tsp garlic powder
- Sea salt and black pepper, to taste
- 1 tsp olive oil
- 1 tbsp fresh lime juice
- 1 small jar of capers in brine

**Instructions:**
1. Place crisper plates into both drawers and lightly coat them with nonstick spray.
2. Combine the salmon with garlic powder, salt, pepper, olive oil, and lime juice, then place them in the cooking basket.
3. Set zone 1 to "AIR FRY" at 190°C for 12 minutes, then use the "MATCH" function to copy the settings to zone 2. Press "START/STOP."
4. At the halfway mark, flip the salmon fillets and scatter capers over them. Close the drawers to continue cooking.
5. Adjust seasoning to taste and serve.

## Parmesan Crusted Tuna

Serves: 4 / Prep time: 10 minutes / Cook time: 17 minutes

**Ingredients:**
- 1 kg tuna steaks
- 1 tsp sweet paprika
- 1 tsp dried parsley
- 1 tsp garlic powder
- Sea salt and black pepper, to taste
- 1 tsp olive oil
- 1 tbsp fresh lime juice
- 150g freshly grated Parmesan cheese

**Instructions:**
1. Place crisper plates in both drawers and coat them with nonstick spray.
2. Season the tuna steaks with paprika, parsley, garlic powder, salt, pepper, olive oil, and lime juice, then place them in the cooking basket.
3. Set zone 1 to "AIR FRY" at 190°C for 17 minutes, using the "MATCH" function to duplicate settings for zone 2. Press "START/STOP."
4. When there are 8 minutes left, flip the tuna steaks and sprinkle Parmesan cheese on top. Close the drawers to continue cooking. Adjust seasoning if needed.

# Sea Scallops

Serves: 4 / Prep time: 5 minutes / Cook time: 7 minutes

### Ingredients:
- 500g jumbo sea scallops, cleaned and dried
- 2 tbsp dry white wine
- 2 tbsp freshly squeezed lemon juice
- 1 tsp garlic powder
- 1 tsp dried basil
- 1 tsp dried rosemary
- Sea salt and black pepper, to taste
- 1 tbsp olive oil
- 1 tsp finely chopped capers
- Sweet chilli sauce, for serving (optional)

### Instructions:
1. Toss the scallops in a mixture of white wine, lemon juice, garlic powder, basil, rosemary, salt, and pepper until well-coated.
2. Place crisper plates in both drawers, then arrange the scallops on the plates.
3. Set zone 1 to "AIR FRY" at 200°C for 7 minutes, using the "MATCH" function to duplicate the settings. Press "START/STOP."
4. Halfway through cooking, shake the basket for even cooking. Close the drawers to resume. Serve with chilli sauce if desired.

# Aromatic Garlic Cod

Serves: 8 / Prep time: 10 minutes / Cook time: 20 minutes

### Ingredients:
- Four large garlic cloves, crushed
- 1 tsp dried rosemary
- 1 tsp dried thyme
- 1 tsp dried sage
- 1 tbsp paprika
- 1200g cod fillets
- Coarse sea salt and black pepper, to taste
- 2 tbsp olive oil

### Instructions:
1. Use a mortar and pestle to crush the garlic, herbs, and spices, then mix with olive oil.
2. Rub this mixture onto the cod fillets.
3. Set zone 1 to "AIR FRY" at 200°C for 11 minutes, then use the "MATCH" function to copy the settings to zone 2. Press "START/STOP."
4. Serve the cod immediately for the best taste.

# Halibut Parcels

Serves: 6 / Prep time: 10 minutes / Cook time: 15 minutes

**Ingredients:**
- Six halibut steaks (about 120g each)
- 2 tsp olive oil
- Three peppers, sliced
- 2 tbsp soy sauce
- 1 tbsp Old Bay seasoning
- Two garlic cloves, chopped
- Six lemon slices
- Six small spring onions, chopped

**Instructions:**
1. Insert crisper plates in both drawers and cut out six 30cm squares of foil, brushing each with olive oil.
2. Toss the halibut and peppers with soy sauce and Old Bay seasoning.
3. Divide the fish, peppers, garlic, and spring onions among the foil squares.
4. Seal the edges of the foil to create parcels, then place them on the crisper plates.
5. Set zone 1 to "AIR FRY" at 200°C for 15 minutes, using the "MATCH" function to copy the settings. Press "START/STOP."
6. At the 8-minute mark, open the foil to allow the steam to escape. Garnish each parcel with a lemon slice and enjoy.

# Fish and Mushroom Patties

Serves: 4-5 / Prep time: 10 minutes / Cook time: 20 minutes

**Ingredients:**
- 1 kg white fish fillets, boneless and flaked
- 200g brown mushrooms, chopped
- Two garlic cloves, minced
- One small leek, chopped
- Two slices of stale bread, crusts removed
- One large egg, beaten
- 2 tbsp finely chopped fresh cilantro
- Sea salt and black pepper, to taste
- 1 tsp smoked paprika
- 100g dried breadcrumbs

**Instructions:**
1. Place crisper plates in both drawers and line them with parchment paper.
2. In a mixing bowl, combine the fish, mushrooms, garlic, leek, bread, egg, cilantro, salt, pepper, and smoked paprika.
3. Shape the mixture into 4-5 patties.
4. Coat each patty with breadcrumbs, pressing them firmly, then arrange them on the crisper plates.
5. Set zone 1 to "AIR FRY" at 200°C for 20 minutes, using the "MATCH" function to copy the settings. Press "START/STOP."
6. Halfway through cooking, flip the patties to ensure even cooking.

# King Prawns with Green Beans

Serves: 3 / Prep time: 30 minutes / Cook time: 15 minutes

### Ingredients:
- Ten raw king prawns, peeled, with tails on
- Juice of 1 lemon
- 2 tbsp soy sauce
- 1 tbsp olive oil
- 1 tbsp Cajun seasoning
- 300g green beans, trimmed
- Sea salt and black pepper, to taste
- 1/2 tsp paprika
- 2 tbsp sesame seeds

### Instructions:
1. Place crisper plates in both drawers and spray with nonstick oil.
2. Marinate the prawns in a mixture of lemon juice, soy sauce, olive oil, and Cajun seasoning for 30 minutes in the fridge.
3. Season the green beans with salt, pepper, and paprika.
4. Place the prawns in zone 1 and the green beans in zone 2, discarding the marinade.
5. Set zone 1 to "AIR FRY" at 200°C for 10 minutes and zone 2 to "AIR FRY" at 200°C for 15 minutes. Use "SYNC" to match the timings, then press "START/STOP."
6. At the halfway point, flip the prawns and stir the green beans.
7. Sprinkle sesame seeds on the beans before serving them with the prawns.

# Cod Fish Croquettes

Serves: 4 / Prep time: 10 minutes / Cook time: 14 minutes

### Ingredients:
- 800g cod fillets, flaked
- One large egg, beaten
- 2 tbsp milk
- One slice of white bread, crust removed
- Two green onions, chopped
- Two garlic cloves, minced
- 2 tbsp finely chopped fresh parsley
- 1 tsp cayenne pepper
- 100g crushed tortilla chips
- Sea salt and black pepper, to taste

### Instructions:
1. Insert crisper plates in both drawers and line them with parchment paper.
2. In a bowl, mix all the Ingredients together until well combined.
3. Shape the mixture into small patties and arrange them on the crisper plates.
4. Set zone 1 to "AIR FRY" at 200°C for 14 minutes, using the "MATCH" function to copy the settings. Press "START/STOP."
5. At the halfway point, flip the croquettes for even cooking.
6. Serve the croquettes warm, paired with a fresh salad.

# Fisherman's Tiger Prawns

Serves: 4 / Prep time: 10 minutes / Cook time: 12 minutes

### Ingredients:
- 600g tiger prawns, deveined and shells removed
- Juice of 1 lemon
- 1 tsp dried rosemary
- 1 tsp dried thyme
- 1 tsp ground black pepper
- 1 tbsp olive oil
- Sea salt, to taste
- Fresh parsley, chopped, for garnish

### Instructions:
1. Place crisper plates in both drawers and coat them with nonstick spray.
2. Toss the prawns in lemon juice, herbs, black pepper, olive oil, and sea salt, then arrange them on the crisper plates.
3. Set zone 1 to "AIR FRY" at 200°C for 12 minutes, using the "MATCH" function to copy the settings. Press "START/STOP."
4. At the halfway point, shake the basket to ensure even cooking.
5. Garnish with parsley and serve.

# Pesto and Olive Crusted Haddock

Serves: 8 / Prep time: 10 minutes / Cook time: 12 minutes

### Ingredients:
- 1200g haddock fillets, skinless (or any firm white fish)
- 200g breadcrumbs
- 4 tbsp green pesto
- 20 green olives, pitted and roughly chopped
- Finely grated zest of 1 large lemon
- Sea salt and ground black pepper, to taste
- 2 tsp olive oil

### Instructions:
1. Pat the fish dry with paper towels.
2. Combine the breadcrumbs, pesto, olives, lemon zest, salt, and pepper until well-mixed. Spread the mixture over the fish fillets.
3. Place the fillets on lightly oiled crisper plates in both zone 1 and zone 2 drawers.
4. Select zone 1, set to "AIR FRY" at 200°C for 12 minutes, then use the "MATCH" function to copy the settings to zone 2. Press "START/STOP."
5. Flip the fillets halfway through the cooking time for even cooking. Serve hot.

# Stuffed Tomatoes with Tuna

Serves: 4 / Prep time: 10 minutes / Cook time: 12 minutes

### Ingredients:
- Four large tomatoes (beefsteak or heirloom)
- 400g canned tuna in oil, drained and flaked
- 100g green olives, pitted and chopped
- 1 large red onion, chopped
- Cracked black pepper, to taste
- 1 tsp garlic granules
- 200g Parmesan cheese, freshly grated

### Instructions:
1. Slice off the tops of the tomatoes and scoop out the seeds and pulp, discarding the cores.
2. In a bowl, mix the tuna, olives, onion, black pepper, and garlic granules. Stuff the tomatoes with the tuna mixture.
3. Place the stuffed tomatoes in both zone 1 and zone 2 drawers.
4. Select zone 1, set to "AIR FRY" at 190°C for 12 minutes, then use the "MATCH" function to copy the settings to zone 2. Press "START/STOP."
5. When there are 6 minutes left, top the tomatoes with Parmesan cheese and continue cooking until fully heated. Serve warm.

# Cajun Garlic Butter Shrimp

Serves: 2 / Prep time: 10 minutes / Cook time: 10 minutes

### Ingredients:
- 300g large shrimp, peeled and deveined
- Two garlic cloves, minced
- 2 tbsp unsalted butter
- 1 tsp Cajun seasoning
- 1/4 tsp smoked paprika
- Salt and pepper, to taste
- Lemon wedges for serving

### Instructions:
1. Preheat the Ninja Dual Zone Air Fryer to 180°C.
2. In a microwave-safe bowl, melt the butter, then stir in the garlic, Cajun seasoning, smoked paprika, salt, and pepper.
3. Toss the shrimp in the butter mixture until well coated.
4. Arrange the shrimp in a single layer on the crisper plate in zone 1.
5. Select "AIR FRY" at 180°C for 10 minutes.
6. Serve the shrimp with lemon wedges.

# Shrimp Scampi with Linguine

Serves: 2 / Prep time: 10 minutes / Cook time: 20 minutes

### Ingredients:
- 225g linguine pasta
- 60ml dry white wine
- 250g large raw shrimp, peeled and deveined
- Three cloves garlic, minced
- 60g unsalted butter
- 60g olive oil
- 1/4 tsp red pepper flakes
- 60ml chicken or vegetable broth
- 60ml freshly squeezed lemon juice
- Salt and freshly ground black pepper to taste
- Fresh parsley, chopped, for garnish

### Instructions:
1. Cook the linguine according to package Instructions, then drain it and set it aside.
2. While the pasta is cooking, prepare the shrimp by mixing them with minced garlic and red pepper flakes.
3. In a skillet, melt the butter with the olive oil over medium heat. Add the shrimp mixture and sauté for 2-3 minutes until the shrimp turn pink and opaque.
4. Pour in the white wine, broth, and lemon juice, stirring until combined. Let the sauce simmer for 2-3 minutes until it thickens slightly.
5. Add the cooked linguine to the skillet, tossing to coat the pasta with the sauce.
6. Season with salt and freshly ground black pepper to taste.
7. Serve hot, garnished with chopped parsley.

# Spiced Sea Bass Parcels

Serves: 4 / Prep time: 25 minutes / Cook time: 12 minutes

### Ingredients:
- Four sea bass fillets
- 2 tbsp olive oil
- 1 tbsp ground cumin
- 1 tbsp ground coriander
- 1 tsp smoked paprika
- 1/2 tsp ground cinnamon
- 1/4 tsp cayenne pepper
- Salt and black pepper, to taste
- Fresh lemon wedges for serving

### Instructions:
1. Preheat the Ninja Dual Zone Air Fryer to 190°C for 5 minutes.
2. In a bowl, mix the olive oil, ground cumin, coriander, smoked paprika, cinnamon, cayenne pepper, salt, and black pepper.
3. Rub the spice mixture onto each sea bass fillet.
4. Wrap each fillet in an individual foil parcel.
5. Place the foil parcels in the air fryer basket.
6. Set to "AIR FRY" at 190°C for 12 minutes or until the sea bass is flaky and cooked through.
7. Serve the sea bass parcels with fresh lemon wedges.

# 4

# Poultry and Meat Recipes

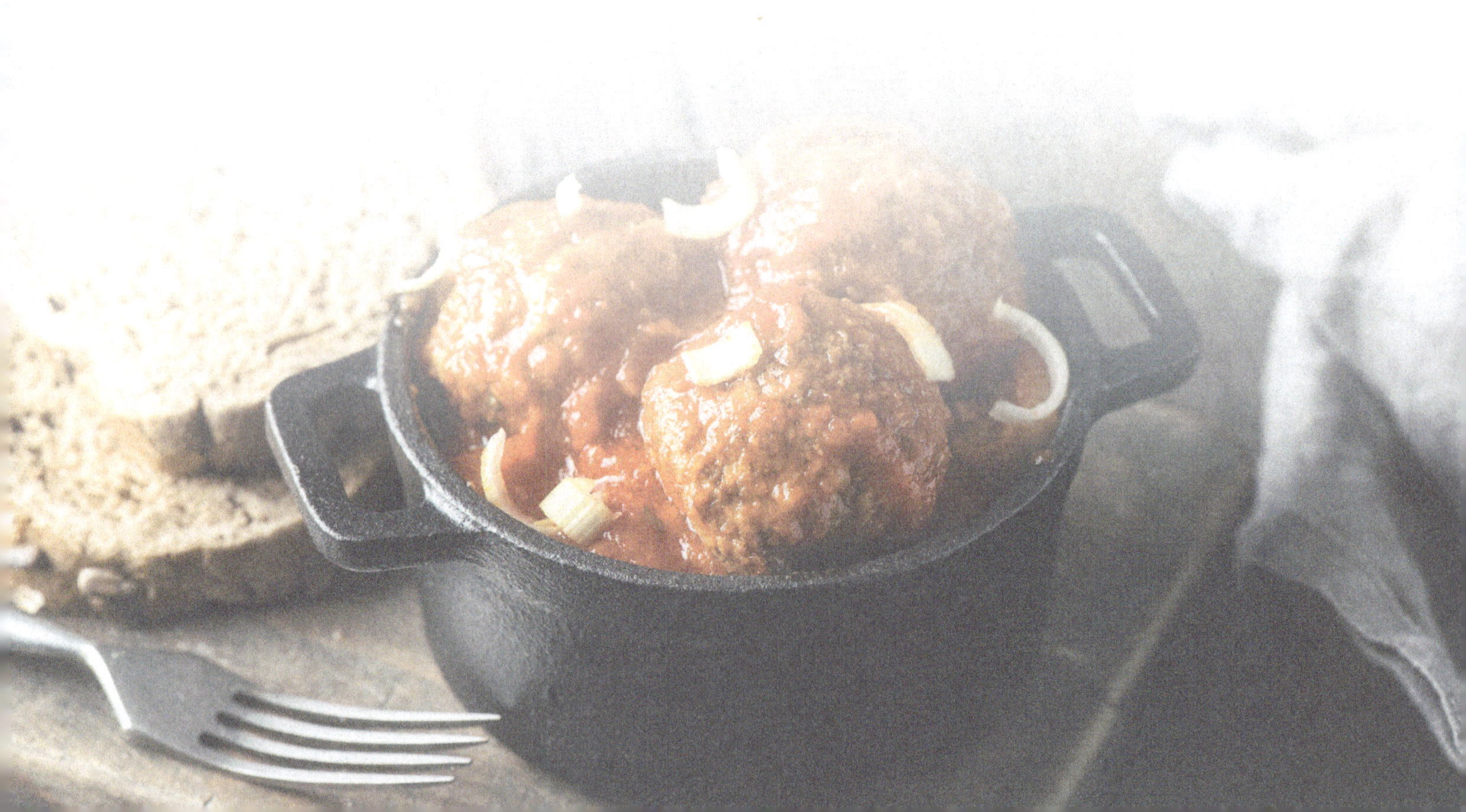

# Mozzarella-Stuffed Pork Medallions

Serves: 4-5 / Prep time: 10 minutes / Cook time: 30 minutes

**Ingredients:**
- 1 kg pork medallions
- A small bunch of sage, leaves picked
- 200g mozzarella ball, sliced into 16 pieces
- Sea salt and cayenne pepper, to taste
- 1 tbsp olive oil

**Instructions:**
1. Cut the pork into two medallions per piece.
2. Place the medallions on a cutting board and carefully create a deep pocket in the side of each with a sharp knife without cutting all the way through.
3. Stuff each pocket with sage leaves and mozzarella slices. Secure the opening with a cocktail stick, then season with salt and cayenne pepper, and brush with olive oil.
4. Place the pork medallions into both drawers of the air fryer.
5. Select zone 1, set to "ROAST" at 180°C for 30 minutes, then use the "MATCH" function to copy the settings to zone 2. Press "START/STOP."
6. When there are 15 minutes remaining, flip the medallions to ensure even browning. Continue cooking until done. Serve hot.

# Chicken with Gnocchi

Serves: 6 / Prep time: 10 minutes / Cook time: 20 minutes

**Ingredients:**
- 1 kg chicken thighs, skinless and boneless
- 2 tsp olive oil
- 1 tbsp paprika
- Sea salt and ground black pepper, to taste
- 400g dry potato gnocchi
- One large red onion, sliced
- 4 tbsp Kalamata olives, pitted and sliced
- 1 tbsp minced garlic
- 200 ml vegetable broth
- Two large tomatoes, chopped
- 200g parmesan cheese, grated

**Instructions:**
1. Cut the chicken thighs into bite-sized pieces and place them in two lightly greased roasting tins. Add the gnocchi, red onion, olives, garlic, vegetable broth, and tomatoes. Stir gently to combine.
2. Place the roasting tins into both drawers of the air fryer.
3. Select zone 1, set to "BAKE" at 195°C for 20 minutes, and use the "MATCH" function to copy the settings to zone 2. Press "START/STOP."
4. When 10 minutes remain, sprinkle the parmesan cheese over the chicken and gnocchi mixture and continue cooking for the remaining time until everything is cooked through and golden. Serve and enjoy!

## Beef Pot Roast

Serves: 4 / Prep time: 10 minutes + marinating time / Cook time: 55 minutes

**Ingredients:**
- 500g rolled beef brisket
- 2 tbsp soy sauce (or coconut aminos)
- 2 tsp vegetable oil
- 100ml red wine
- Two bay leaves
- 1 tsp hot paprika
- 1 tsp dried parsley flakes
- 2 tbsp corn flour
- Sea salt and ground black pepper, to taste
- One celery root, peeled and cut into bite-sized pieces
- One large carrot, trimmed and cut into bite-sized pieces
- Two peppers, deseeded and halved
- Two small onions, peeled and halved

**Instructions:**
1. Marinate the beef brisket in soy sauce, oil, wine, bay leaves, paprika, parsley, salt, and pepper in a ceramic dish. Cover and refrigerate for about 2 hours. Reserve the marinade.
2. Toss the marinated beef with corn flour and one teaspoon of vegetable oil. Place the beef in a lightly greased baking tin.
3. Toss the vegetables with one teaspoon of vegetable oil, salt, and pepper. Add them to a separate lightly greased baking tin, covering it with foil (shiny side down). Place both tins in the air fryer drawers.
4. Select zone 1, set to "AIR FRY" at 180°C for 45 minutes, and select zone 2 to "ROAST" at 190°C for 12 minutes. Use the "SYNC" function to synchronise the cooking time. Press "START/STOP."
5. After 20 minutes, flip the beef in zone 1 to ensure even cooking.
6. When there are 6 minutes left in zone 2, toss the vegetables to ensure even roasting.
7. While the beef and vegetables cook, gently simmer the reserved marinade over medium-high heat until it thickens into a sauce.
8. Serve the beef brisket with the roasted vegetables and drizzle the sauce on top.

## Rosemary and Garlic Air-Fried Lamb Chops

Serves: 4 / Prep time: 15 minutes / Cook time: 12 minutes

**Ingredients:**
- Four lamb chops
- Two cloves garlic, minced
- 2 tbsp olive oil
- 1 tbsp fresh rosemary, chopped
- Salt and black pepper, to taste
- Lemon wedges for serving

**Instructions:**
1. Preheat the Ninja Dual Zone Air Fryer to 200°C for 5 minutes.
2. In a bowl, mix the olive oil, minced garlic, chopped rosemary, salt, and black pepper.
3. Coat each lamb chop with the garlic and rosemary mixture.
4. Place the lamb chops in the air fryer basket.
5. Air fry at 200°C for 12 minutes or until the lamb is cooked to your desired doneness.
6. Serve the lamb chops with lemon wedges for an added zest.

# Rotisserie-Style Roast Chicken

Serves: 6 / Prep time: 10 minutes / Cook time: 16 minutes

### Ingredients:
- 1.2kg chicken breasts, skinless and boneless
- 1 tsp Italian spice mix
- Two garlic cloves, smashed
- Sea salt and ground black pepper, to taste
- 2 tbsp olive oil

### Instructions:
1. Rub the chicken breasts with the Italian spice mix, garlic, salt, pepper, and olive oil until well coated on all sides.
2. Place the seasoned chicken breasts into both air fryer drawers.
3. Select zone 1, set to "BAKE" at 200°C for 16 minutes, and use the "MATCH" function to duplicate the settings in zone 2. Press "START/STOP."
4. Once cooked, transfer the chicken to a cutting board and let it rest for about 10 minutes before carving and serving.
5. Enjoy the tender and flavorful roast chicken.

# Paprika Pork Medallions

Serves: 4-5 / Prep time: 5 minutes / Cook time: 25 minutes

### Ingredients:
- 800g pork medallions
- 1 tbsp butter, melted
- 1 tbsp hot paprika
- 1/2 tsp onion powder
- 1/2 tsp garlic granules
- 1 tbsp sunflower oil
- Sea salt and ground black pepper, to taste

### Instructions:
1. Insert crisper plates into both air fryer drawers and spray them with nonstick cooking spray.
2. Toss the pork medallions with melted butter, paprika, onion powder, garlic granules, sunflower oil, salt, and pepper until well coated.
3. Place the seasoned pork medallions in the cooking baskets.
4. Select zone 1, set to "AIR FRY" at 200°C for 25 minutes, and use the "MATCH" function to duplicate settings to zone 2. Press "START/STOP."
5. Flip the pork medallions halfway through the cooking time to ensure even cooking. Serve hot.

## Thai Basil Chicken

Serves: 4 / Prep time: 15 minutes / Cook time: 10 minutes

**Ingredients:**
- 500g boneless, skinless chicken thighs cut into bite-sized pieces
- 2 tbsp soy sauce
- 1 tbsp oyster sauce
- 1 tbsp fish sauce
- 2 tsp sugar
- Two cloves garlic, minced
- One red chilli, sliced (adjust to taste)
- 1 cup fresh basil leaves
- 2 tbsp vegetable oil

**Instructions:**
1. In a bowl, mix together the soy sauce, oyster sauce, fish sauce, sugar, minced garlic, and sliced chilli.
2. Add the chicken pieces and toss to coat. Let it marinate for 10 minutes.
3. Preheat the Ninja Dual Zone Air Fryer to 200°C in zone 1 for 5 minutes.
4. Remove the chicken from the marinade and shake off any excess.
5. Place the chicken in zone 1 of the air fryer and cook at 200°C for 8-10 minutes or until cooked through and slightly browned.
6. Heat vegetable oil in a pan over medium heat. Add the cooked chicken and basil leaves, stir-frying for an additional minute until the basil wilts.
7. Serve the Thai basil chicken with steamed rice or noodles. Enjoy!

## Korean BBQ Beef Short Ribs

Serves: 4 / Prep time: 20 minutes / Cook time: 10 minutes

**Ingredients:**
- 800g beef short ribs
- 4 tbsp soy sauce
- 2 tbsp brown sugar
- 2 tbsp sesame oil
- Two cloves garlic, minced
- 1 tbsp grated ginger
- 1 tbsp rice vinegar
- 1 tsp toasted sesame seeds
- Two green onions, chopped
- Salt and black pepper, to taste

**Instructions:**
1. Preheat the Ninja Dual Zone Air Fryer to 200°C in zone 1 for 5 minutes.
2. In a bowl, mix the soy sauce, brown sugar, sesame oil, minced garlic, grated ginger, rice vinegar, toasted sesame seeds, chopped green onions, salt, and pepper to make a marinade.
3. Place the beef short ribs in a shallow dish and pour the marinade over them, making sure they are evenly coated. Marinate for 20 minutes.
4. Remove the ribs from the marinade, allowing any excess to drip off.
5. Place the ribs in zone 1 of the air fryer and cook at 200°C for 8-10 minutes or until they reach your desired level of doneness.
6. Let the beef short ribs rest for a few minutes before serving.
7. Serve hot with steamed rice, kimchi, and fresh lettuce leaves for wrapping. Enjoy!

# Brazilian Picanha Steak

Serves: 4 / Prep time: 10 minutes / Cook time: 15 minutes

**Ingredients:**
- 800g picanha steak (rump cap or sirloin cap)
- 2 tbsp coarse sea salt
- 1 tbsp vegetable oil
- Chimichurri sauce for serving (optional)

**Instructions:**
1. Preheat the Ninja Dual Zone Air Fryer to 200°C in zone 1 for 5 minutes.
2. Sprinkle the coarse sea salt evenly over the picanha steak, pressing it gently into the meat.
3. Drizzle the steak with vegetable oil and place it in zone 1 of the air fryer.
4. Cook at 200°C for 12-15 minutes, flipping halfway through, or until it reaches your desired level of doneness.
5. Remove the steak and let it rest for a few minutes before slicing.
6. Serve with chimichurri sauce if desired. Enjoy!

# Chinese Honey Sesame Chicken

Serves: 4 / Prep time: 15 minutes / Cook time: 12 minutes

**Ingredients:**
- 500g boneless, skinless chicken thighs cut into bite-sized pieces
- 3 tbsp soy sauce
- 2 tbsp honey
- 2 tbsp hoisin sauce
- 1 tbsp rice vinegar
- Two cloves garlic, minced
- 1 tsp grated fresh ginger
- 1 tsp sesame oil
- 1 tbsp cornstarch
- 2 tbsp water
- 1 tbsp sesame seeds, for garnish
- Sliced green onions for garnish

**Instructions:**
1. Preheat the Ninja Dual Zone Air Fryer to 200°C in zone 1 for 5 minutes.
2. In a bowl, mix the soy sauce, honey, hoisin sauce, rice vinegar, minced garlic, grated ginger, and sesame oil to make the sauce.
3. Coat the chicken pieces with half of the sauce and set the rest aside.
4. Place the chicken in zone 1 of the air fryer in a single layer. Air fry at 200°C for 10-12 minutes, shaking or flipping halfway through.
5. While the chicken cooks, mix the cornstarch with water to make a slurry.
6. Heat the remaining sauce in a saucepan, whisk in the cornstarch slurry, and cook until thickened.
7. Toss the cooked chicken with the thickened sauce.
8. Garnish with sesame seeds and sliced green onions. Serve with steamed rice and stir-fried vegetables. Enjoy!

# Breaded Veal Cutlets

Serves: 4 / Prep time: 15 minutes / Cook time: 12 minutes

**Ingredients:**
- Four veal cutlets (about 150g each)
- 120g breadcrumbs
- 50g grated Parmesan cheese
- 1 tsp dried parsley
- 1/2 tsp garlic powder
- Salt and black pepper, to taste
- Two large eggs, beaten
- 60 ml milk
- Vegetable oil, for frying

**Instructions:**
1. Preheat the Ninja Dual Zone Air Fryer to 200°C in zone 1 for 5 minutes.
2. In a shallow dish, combine breadcrumbs, Parmesan cheese, dried parsley, garlic powder, salt, and pepper.
3. In another bowl, whisk together the beaten eggs and milk.
4. Coat each veal cutlet in the breadcrumb mixture, then dip into the egg mixture, and coat again with breadcrumbs.
5. Place the breaded cutlets in zone 1 of the air fryer and drizzle with vegetable oil.
6. Air fry at 200°C for 12 minutes, flipping halfway through, until golden and cooked through.
7. Let the cutlets rest on a wire rack for a few minutes before serving. Enjoy with lemon wedges, mashed potatoes or pasta, and a fresh green salad.

# Mediterranean Poultry Salad

Serves: 6 / Prep time: 10 minutes / Cook time: 20 minutes

**Ingredients:**
- 800g chicken breasts
- 2 tbsp extra-virgin olive oil
- Sea salt and ground black pepper, to taste
- One large red onion
- 1 tbsp red wine vinegar
- One small Persian cucumber, sliced
- One medium head of red cabbage, shredded

**Instructions:**
1. Toss the chicken and onion with one tablespoon of olive oil, salt, and pepper. Place the chicken in zone 1 of the air fryer and the onion in zone 2.
2. Set zone 1 to "AIR FRY" at 200°C for 20 minutes and zone 2 to "ROAST" at 180°C for 10 minutes. Select "SYNC" and press "START/STOP."
3. In a bowl, mix the chicken with the cucumber and shredded cabbage. Whisk together the remaining olive oil, vinegar, salt, and pepper for the dressing.
4. Toss the salad with the dressing and enjoy!

# Mediterranean Herb Chicken Pasta Bake

Serves: 4 / Prep time: 10 minutes / Cook time: 24 minutes

## Ingredients:
- 250g dry whole-wheat pasta
- 2 tbsp olive oil
- 800g chicken breasts, skinless, sliced into strips
- One large onion, finely chopped
- Two cloves garlic, crushed
- 2 (400g) cans chopped tomatoes
- 1 tsp Aleppo pepper
- Sea salt and ground black pepper, to taste
- 1 tbsp fresh parsley, chopped
- 1 tbsp fresh coriander, chopped
- 200g Provolone cheese, grated

## Instructions:
1. Remove a crisper plate from your air fryer and brush two baking tins with nonstick oil.
2. Cook the pasta according to package Instructions.
3. Meanwhile, heat olive oil in a pan over medium-high heat and cook the chicken until no longer pink, about 4 minutes.
4. Combine the cooked chicken with the pasta, onion, garlic, tomatoes, Aleppo pepper, salt, pepper, and 100g of cheese. Divide the mixture between the prepared baking tins.
5. Place the tins in the air fryer. Select zone 1, set to "BAKE" at 180°C for 20 minutes, and use the "MATCH" function to copy the settings to zone 2. Press "START/STOP."
6. When there are 10 minutes left, sprinkle the remaining cheese on top and continue baking until bubbly and golden. Enjoy!

# Rosemary Garlic Air Fryer Lamb Steaks

Serves: 2 / Prep time: 35 minutes / Cook time: 16 minutes

## Ingredients:
- Two lamb steaks (about 200g each)
- 30 ml olive oil
- Two cloves garlic, minced
- 15 ml lemon juice
- 5 g fresh rosemary leaves, chopped
- 5 g salt
- 2 g black pepper
- Cooking spray or oil for greasing the air fryer basket

## Instructions:
1. Mix olive oil, minced garlic, lemon juice, chopped rosemary, salt, and pepper to create a marinade.
2. Coat the lamb steaks with the marinade and let them sit at room temperature for 30 minutes or refrigerate for a few hours.
3. Preheat the air fryer to 200°C for 5 minutes.
4. Lightly grease the air fryer basket.
5. Place the marinated lamb steaks in a single layer in the basket.
6. Air fry at 200°C for 8-10 minutes for medium-rare, flipping halfway through. Adjust cooking time for your preferred doneness.
7. Let the lamb rest for a few minutes before slicing. Serve as a main course. Enjoy!

# Beef Sandwiches

Serves: 6 / Prep time: 10 minutes / Cook time: 20 minutes

### Ingredients:
- 600g sirloin steak, sliced
- 600g peppers, deseeded and halved
- 1 tbsp extra-virgin olive oil
- Two garlic cloves, crushed
- Sea salt and ground black pepper, to taste
- One large tomato, diced
- One medium onion, sliced
- Six sandwich rolls, split

### Instructions:
1. Toss the steak and bell peppers with olive oil, garlic, salt, and pepper.
2. Place the steak in zone 1 and the bell peppers in zone 2 of the air fryer.
3. Set zone 1 to "ROAST" at 195°C for 20 minutes and zone 2 to "ROAST" at 190°C for 10 minutes. Select "SYNC" and press "START/STOP."
4. Flip the steak and peppers halfway through cooking.
5. Slice the steak into bite-sized strips. Assemble sandwiches with the rolls, tomato, and onion. Enjoy!

# BBQ Pulled Pork Loaded Potato Skins

Serves: 4 / Prep time: 15 minutes / Cook time: 25 minutes

### Ingredients:
- Four large baking potatoes, scrubbed
- 300g pulled pork (pre-cooked)
- 100g shredded cheddar cheese
- 4 tbsp BBQ sauce
- Two spring onions, chopped
- Salt and black pepper, to taste
- Sour cream (for serving)

### Instructions:
1. Preheat the Ninja Dual Zone Air Fryer to 200°C for 5 minutes.
2. Pierce each potato with a fork and microwave for 10 minutes or until partially cooked.
3. Cut the potatoes in half lengthwise and scoop out the flesh, leaving a thin potato skin.
4. In one zone, air fry the potato skins until crispy.
5. In the other zone, heat the pulled pork with BBQ sauce until warmed through.
6. Fill each crispy potato skin with the BBQ-pulled pork mixture.
7. Top with shredded cheddar cheese and air fry for another 5 minutes until the cheese is melted and bubbly.
8. Garnish with spring onions, season with salt and pepper, and serve with a dollop of sour cream. Enjoy!

# 5
# Healthy Vegetables and Sides

# Parmesan Roast Asparagus

Serves: 5 / Prep time: 10 minutes / Cook time: 14 minutes

### Ingredients:
- 1 kg asparagus spears, trimmed
- 2 tbsp butter, melted
- 1 tsp garlic granules
- 1 tsp hot paprika
- Sea salt and ground black pepper, to taste
- One small lemon
- 100g Parmesan cheese, grated

### Instructions:
1. Toss the asparagus spears in a bowl with melted butter, garlic granules, hot paprika, sea salt, and black pepper.
2. Place the asparagus in both drawers of your Ninja Foodi air fryer, making sure a crisper plate is inserted.
3. Set zone 1 to "AIR FRY" at 200°C for 14 minutes. Select "MATCH" and press "START/STOP" to begin.
4. Halfway through cooking, sprinkle the asparagus with grated Parmesan cheese. Reinsert the drawers to continue cooking.
5. Serve the roasted asparagus with a squeeze of fresh lemon juice. Enjoy!

# Cheesy Cauliflower Bites with Yoghurt Dip

Serves: 4 / Prep time: 15 minutes / Cook time: 15 minutes

### Ingredients:
- 400g cauliflower florets
- 100g breadcrumbs
- 100g grated cheddar cheese
- 2 eggs, beaten
- 1 tsp garlic powder
- 1 tsp onion powder
- Salt and black pepper, to taste
- Olive oil, for greasing

### Instructions:
1. Preheat the Ninja Dual Zone Air Fryer to 190°C for 5 minutes.
2. In a bowl, mix the cauliflower florets with breadcrumbs, grated cheddar, beaten eggs, garlic powder, onion powder, salt, and black pepper until well combined.
3. Shape the mixture into bite-sized cauliflower balls.
4. Lightly grease the air fryer baskets with olive oil, then place the cauliflower bites inside.
5. Air fry at 190°C for 15 minutes or until golden brown and crispy.
6. Serve the cheesy cauliflower bites hot with a refreshing yoghurt dip. Enjoy!

# Curry-Spiced Squash Rings

Serves: 4 / Prep time: 10 minutes / Cook time: 15 minutes

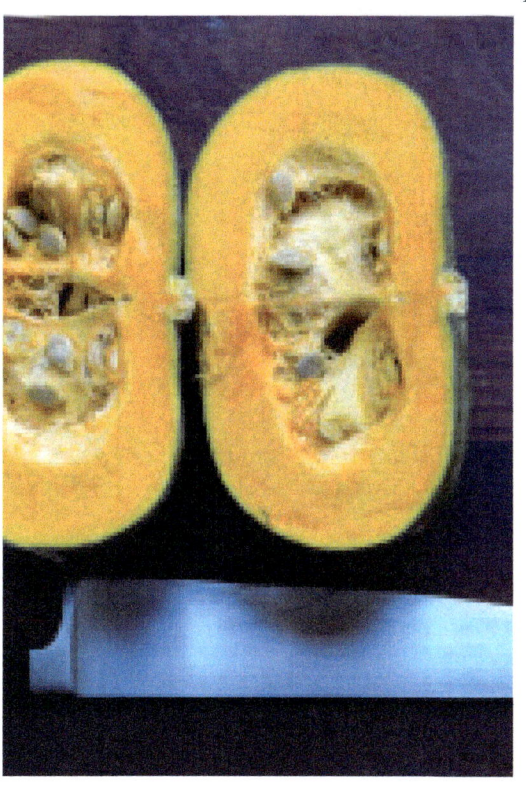

**Ingredients:**
- One small acorn squash, sliced into rings
- 2 tbsp olive oil
- 1 tsp curry powder
- 1/2 tsp ground cumin
- 1/2 tsp turmeric
- 1/4 tsp cayenne pepper
- Salt and black pepper, to taste
- Fresh coriander, for garnish (optional)

**Instructions:**
1. Preheat the Ninja Dual Zone Air Fryer to 190°C for 5 minutes.
2. Toss the squash rings in a bowl with olive oil, curry powder, cumin, turmeric, cayenne pepper, salt, and black pepper until evenly coated.
3. Arrange the seasoned squash rings in the air fryer baskets.
4. Air fry at 190°C for 15 minutes or until the squash is tender and slightly crispy.
5. Garnish with fresh coriander, if desired, and serve as a unique, flavorful side dish. Enjoy!

# Crispy Brussels Sprouts with Maple Glaze

Serves: 2 / Prep time: 10 minutes / Cook time: 20 minutes

**Ingredients:**
- 300g Brussels sprouts, trimmed and halved
- 1 tbsp olive oil
- Salt and pepper, to taste
- 2 tbsp maple syrup
- 1 tbsp soy sauce
- 1 tbsp balsamic vinegar
- One garlic clove, minced
- 1/4 tsp red pepper flakes

**Instructions:**
1. Preheat the Ninja Dual Zone Air Fryer to 200°C.
2. Toss the Brussels sprouts in a bowl with olive oil, salt, and pepper.
3. Place the Brussels sprouts in zone 1 of the air fryer and select "AIR FRY" for 10 minutes.
4. Meanwhile, mix the maple syrup, soy sauce, balsamic vinegar, minced garlic, and red pepper flakes in a small bowl.
5. After 10 minutes, open zone 1 and brush the Brussels sprouts with the maple glaze.
6. Move the air fryer basket to zone 2 and continue to "AIR FRY" for another 10 minutes or until the Brussels sprouts are crispy and caramelised. Serve immediately. Enjoy!

# Crispy Kale Chips with Smoked Paprika

Serves: 2 / Prep time: 5 minutes / Cook time: 8 minutes

**Ingredients:**
- 150g kale, stems removed and torn into bite-size pieces
- 1 tbsp olive oil
- 1/2 tsp smoked paprika
- Salt, to taste

**Instructions:**
1. Preheat the Ninja Dual Zone Air Fryer to 160°C using the "AIR FRY" function.
2. Toss the kale pieces in a bowl with olive oil, smoked paprika, and salt until evenly coated.
3. Arrange the seasoned kale in a single layer on the crisper plate.
4. Set zone 1 to "AIR FRY" at 160°C for 8 minutes. Press "START/STOP" to begin.
5. After 4 minutes, pause the cooking and flip the kale pieces using tongs. Close the air fryer and continue cooking.
6. Once done, remove the crispy kale chips and serve immediately. Enjoy!

# Glazed Root Vegetables

Serves: 6 / Prep time: 10 minutes / Cook time: 20 minutes

**Ingredients:**
- 300g carrots, cut into sticks
- 200g parsnips, cut into sticks
- 200g red beets, peeled and cut into sticks
- 2 tbsp butter, melted
- 2 tbsp sherry vinegar
- 1 tsp cayenne pepper
- Sea salt and black pepper, to taste
- 2 tbsp maple syrup

**Instructions:**
1. Preheat the Ninja Dual Zone Air Fryer to 180°C.
2. Toss the carrots, parsnips, and beets in a large bowl with melted butter, sherry vinegar, cayenne pepper, salt, and black pepper.
3. Divide the vegetables between two roasting tins and place them in both zones of the air fryer.
4. Select zone 1 and set it to "ROAST" at 180°C for 20 minutes. Select "MATCH" to duplicate the settings in zone 2, then press "START/STOP."
5. After 10 minutes, toss the vegetables with maple syrup and return the tins to the air fryer to continue cooking. Enjoy!

# Vegan Air Fryer Falafel

Serves: 4 / Prep time: 12 minutes / Cook time: 25 minutes

**Ingredients:**
- Two cans of chickpeas, drained and rinsed
- 1/2 red onion (60g), finely chopped
- 120ml parsley, chopped
- 120ml cilantro, chopped
- 30g flour
- 1 tsp cumin
- 1 tsp coriander
- 1/2 tsp salt
- 1/4 tsp black pepper
- Cooking spray

**Instructions:**
1. Preheat the Ninja Dual Zone Air Fryer to 190°C.
2. In a food processor, pulse the chickpeas, red onion, parsley, cilantro, flour, cumin, coriander, salt, and black pepper until finely chopped but not pureed.
3. Shape the mixture into small balls.
4. Lightly spray the air fryer basket with cooking spray and place the falafel balls inside in a single layer.
5. Air fry for 10-12 minutes or until golden brown and crispy.
6. Repeat the process until all falafel balls are cooked.
7. Serve with hummus, pita bread, and fresh vegetables. Enjoy!

# Butternut Squash Wedges

Serves: 4 / Prep time: 10 minutes / Cook time: 20 minutes

**Ingredients:**
- 600g butternut squash, peeled and cut into wedges
- 2 tbsp olive oil
- 1 tsp smoked paprika
- 1/2 tsp ground cumin
- Salt and black pepper, to taste

**Instructions:**
1. Preheat the Ninja Dual Zone Air Fryer to 200°C in zone 1 for 5 minutes.
2. Toss the butternut squash wedges in a bowl with olive oil, smoked paprika, ground cumin, salt, and black pepper until well coated.
3. Place the seasoned wedges in zone 1 of the air fryer.
4. Cook at 200°C for 20 minutes, shaking the basket halfway through, until tender and lightly browned.
5. Allow the wedges to cool slightly before serving. Enjoy the sweet and savoury flavours!

## Turmeric-Roasted Chickpeas

Serves: 4 / Prep time: 5 minutes / Cook time: 20 minutes

### Ingredients:
- 400g can chickpeas, drained and rinsed
- 1 tbsp olive oil
- 1 tsp ground turmeric
- 1/2 tsp smoked paprika
- 1/2 tsp garlic powder
- Sea salt, to taste

### Instructions:
1. Preheat the Ninja Dual Zone Air Fryer to 200°C using the "ROAST" function.
2. Toss the chickpeas in a bowl with olive oil, turmeric, smoked paprika, garlic powder, and sea salt until well coated.
3. Spread the chickpeas evenly on the crisper plate in zone 1.
4. Roast for 20 minutes, shaking the crisper plate halfway through.
5. Serve hot as a snack, or add to your favourite salad for extra crunch. Enjoy!

## Grilled Portobello Mushrooms

Serves: 4 / Prep time: 10 minutes / Cook time: 10 minutes

### Ingredients:
- Four large Portobello mushrooms
- 2 tbsp balsamic vinegar
- 2 tbsp olive oil
- Two cloves garlic, minced
- Salt and black pepper, to taste

### Instructions:
1. Preheat the Ninja Dual Zone Air Fryer to 200°C in zone 1 for 5 minutes.
2. In a bowl, whisk together balsamic vinegar, olive oil, minced garlic, salt, and black pepper.
3. Place the mushrooms in a shallow dish and pour the marinade over them, ensuring all sides are coated. Let marinate for 5 minutes.
4. Place the mushrooms in zone 1 of the air fryer.
5. Cook at 200°C for 10 minutes, flipping halfway through, until tender and slightly charred.
6. Let the mushrooms cool slightly before serving. Enjoy the meaty texture and tangy flavour!

# Warm Herbed Cannellini Bean Salad

Serves: 4 / Prep time: 15 minutes / Cook time: 5 minutes

**Ingredients:**
- 400g canned cannellini beans, drained and rinsed
- One cucumber, diced
- 200g cherry tomatoes, halved
- 50g fresh mint, chopped
- 60g fresh parsley, chopped
- 100g feta cheese, crumbled
- 2 tbsp extra virgin olive oil
- 1 tbsp red wine vinegar
- Salt and black pepper, to taste

**Instructions:**
1. In a large bowl, combine cannellini beans, diced cucumber, cherry tomatoes, mint, parsley, and crumbled feta.
2. In a small bowl, whisk together extra virgin olive oil, red wine vinegar, salt, and black pepper to make the dressing.
3. Drizzle the dressing over the bean mixture and toss gently to combine.
4. Warm the salad in the Ninja Dual Zone Air Fryer at a low temperature for 5 minutes.
5. Serve immediately, enjoying the warm and flavorful combination, or refrigerate until ready to serve. Enjoy a fresh and vibrant salad!

# Sesame Soy Broccoli

Serves: 4 / Prep time: 10 minutes / Cook time: 8 minutes

**Ingredients:**
- 500g broccoli florets
- 2 tbsp soy sauce
- 1 tbsp sesame oil
- 1 tbsp sesame seeds
- Two cloves garlic, minced
- Salt and black pepper, to taste

**Instructions:**
1. Preheat the Ninja Dual Zone Air Fryer to 200°C in zone 1 for 5 minutes.
2. In a bowl, whisk together soy sauce, sesame oil, sesame seeds, minced garlic, salt, and black pepper.
3. Place the broccoli florets in a shallow dish and pour the marinade over them, ensuring they are evenly coated.
4. Let the broccoli marinate for 5 minutes.
5. Place the marinated broccoli in zone 1 of the air fryer.
6. Cook at 200°C for 8 minutes, shaking the basket halfway through, until the broccoli is tender-crisp and slightly charred.
7. Remove the sesame soy broccoli from the air fryer and let it cool for a few minutes.
8. Serve as a tasty and healthy side dish, enjoying the nutty sesame and savoury soy flavours. Enjoy!

# Spicy Okra

Serves: 4 / Prep time: 10 minutes / Cook time: 12 minutes

## Ingredients:
- 300g okra, trimmed and halved lengthwise
- 2 tbsp olive oil
- 1/2 tsp ground cumin
- 1/2 tsp paprika
- 1/4 tsp cayenne pepper (adjust to taste)
- Salt and black pepper, to taste

## Instructions:
1. Preheat the Ninja Dual Zone Air Fryer to 200°C in zone 1 for 5 minutes.
2. In a bowl, toss the okra with olive oil, ground cumin, paprika, cayenne pepper, salt, and black pepper until well coated.
3. Place the seasoned okra in zone 1 of the air fryer.
4. Cook at 200°C for 12 minutes, shaking the basket halfway through, until the okra is tender-crisp and lightly browned.
5. Remove the spicy okra from the air fryer and let it cool for a few minutes.
6. Serve as a flavorful side dish or snack, enjoying the satisfying crunch and spice. Enjoy!

# Baked Potatoes

Serves: 4 / Prep time: 5 minutes / Cook time: 40 minutes

## Ingredients:
- Four medium-sized potatoes
- Olive oil for brushing
- Salt, to taste
- Toppings of your choice (e.g., sour cream, chives, grated cheese)

## Instructions:
1. Preheat the Ninja Dual Zone Air Fryer to 200°C in zone 1 for 5 minutes.
2. Wash and dry the potatoes. Prick each potato several times with a fork.
3. Brush the potatoes with olive oil and sprinkle with salt.
4. Place the potatoes in zone 1 of the air fryer, leaving space between them.
5. Cook at 200°C for 40-45 minutes, until tender with crispy skins.
6. Remove the baked potatoes from the air fryer and let them cool for a few minutes.
7. Cut a slit in each potato, fluff the insides with a fork, and add your favourite toppings. Enjoy a comforting and versatile dish!

# Crab-Stuffed Mushrooms

Serves: 4 / Prep time: 10 minutes / Cook time: 15 minutes

## Ingredients:
- 12 large button mushrooms
- One small onion, finely chopped
- One garlic clove, minced
- 1 tbsp chopped fresh parsley
- Salt and black pepper, to taste
- 2 tbsp grated Parmesan cheese
- 200g fresh crab meat
- 2 tbsp cream cheese
- 1 tbsp lemon juice
- 1 tbsp olive oil

## Instructions:
1. Preheat the Ninja Dual Zone Air Fryer to 180°C using the Roast function.
2. Wipe the mushrooms clean with a damp cloth and remove the stems.
3. Heat olive oil in a pan and sauté the onions until soft. Add the minced garlic and cook for another minute.
4. Stir in the crab meat, cream cheese, parsley, lemon juice, salt, and pepper. Mix well.
5. Spoon the crab mixture into the mushroom caps and sprinkle with grated Parmesan cheese.
6. Place the stuffed mushrooms onto the crisper plate in zone 1 of the air fryer.
7. Roast at 180°C for 10-15 minutes until the cheese is melted and the mushrooms are tender. Enjoy a delightful seafood appetisers!

# Candied Yams with Marshmallows and Pecans

Serves: 6 / Prep time: 15 minutes / Cook time: 25 minutes

## Ingredients:
- Four medium yams peeled and cut into 1-inch cubes
- 50g unsalted butter, melted
- 1/2 tsp ground cinnamon
- 1/4 tsp salt
- 100g mini marshmallows
- 50g brown sugar
- 1/4 tsp ground nutmeg
- 50g chopped pecans

## Instructions:
1. Preheat the Ninja Dual Zone Air Fryer to 180°C.
2. In a large bowl, toss the yams with melted butter, brown sugar, cinnamon, nutmeg, and salt.
3. Arrange the yams in a single layer in zone 1 of the air fryer.
4. Cook at 180°C for 20 minutes, stirring halfway through.
5. In a small bowl, mix together the pecans and marshmallows.
6. Sprinkle the pecan and marshmallow mixture over the yams.
7. Move the yams to zone 2 of the air fryer and cook for an additional 5 minutes until the marshmallows are golden brown and toasted.
8. Serve hot, and enjoy this sweet and crunchy side dish!

# Tandoori Vegetable Skewers

Serves: 4 / Prep time: 20 minutes (+ Marinating time: 1-2 hours) / Cook time: 15 minutes

### Ingredients:
- One large red pepper, cut into chunks
- One large yellow pepper, cut into chunks
- One large green pepper, cut into chunks
- One medium red onion, cut into chunks
- One medium zucchini, sliced into thick rounds
- One medium eggplant, cut into chunks
- 240ml plain Greek yoghurt
- 2 tbsp tandoori masala powder
- 2 tbsp lemon juice
- 2 tbsp olive oil
- Two cloves garlic, minced
- 1 tsp ground cumin
- 1 tsp ground coriander
- 1/2 tsp turmeric powder
- 1/2 tsp paprika
- Salt and pepper, to taste
- Optional: Fresh cilantro for garnish

### Instructions:
1. Preheat the Ninja Dual Zone Air Fryer to 200°C using the "AIR FRY" mode.
2. In a bowl, mix Greek yoghurt, tandoori masala powder, lemon juice, olive oil, minced garlic, cumin, coriander, turmeric, paprika, salt, and pepper to make the marinade.
3. Add the bell peppers, red onion, zucchini, and eggplant to the marinade, tossing to coat evenly. Marinate in the refrigerator for 1-2 hours.
4. Thread the marinated vegetables onto skewers, alternating between different vegetables.
5. Place the skewers in the lower zone of the air fryer. Cook for 12-15 minutes, flipping halfway through, until the vegetables are tender and slightly charred.
6. Garnish with fresh cilantro, if desired, and serve. Enjoy the vibrant flavours!

# 6
# Appetisers

# Mini Pizza Rolls

Serves: 4 / Prep time: 15 minutes / Cook Time: 10 minutes

**Ingredients:**
- One sheet of puff pastry, rolled out and sliced into strips
- 200g pizza sauce
- 150g shredded mozzarella cheese
- 50g pepperoni slices
- 1 tsp dried oregano
- 1 tsp dried basil
- 1/2 tsp garlic powder

**Preparation Instructions:**
1. Preheat the Ninja Dual Zone Air Fryer's second zone to 200°C for 5 minutes.
2. Lay the puff pastry strips on a clean surface.
3. At one end of each strip, place a spoonful of pizza sauce, followed by mozzarella, pepperoni, oregano, basil, and garlic powder.
4. Roll the pastry over the filling, forming tight rolls.
5. Place the pizza rolls in the second zone of the air fryer basket.
6. Air fry at 200°C for 10 minutes or until the rolls are golden brown.
7. Serve the mini pizza rolls warm.

# Garlic Herb Croutons

Serves: 4 / Prep time: 10 minutes / Cook Time: 15 minutes

**Ingredients:**
- Four slices of bread (white, brown, or sourdough)
- Two cloves garlic, finely minced
- 2 tbsp olive oil
- 1 tbsp dried mixed herbs (such as oregano, thyme, and rosemary)
- Salt and black pepper to taste

**Preparation Instructions:**
1. Preheat the Ninja Dual Zone Air Fryer to 180°C on the "BAKE" setting.
2. Cut the bread into small cubes and place them in a bowl.
3. Add minced garlic, olive oil, mixed herbs, salt, and black pepper, tossing until the bread is evenly coated.
4. Transfer the seasoned bread cubes to the crisper basket of the air fryer.
5. Set zone 1 to "BAKE" at 180°C for 10 minutes and zone 2 to "BAKE" at 180°C for 15 minutes. Press "SYNC" and then the "START/STOP" button.
6. Halfway through, shake the basket to ensure even cooking.
7. Once done, remove the croutons from the air fryer and let them cool before serving.

# Sausage Patty Sliders

Serves: 12 / Prep time: 5 minutes / Cook Time: 8 minutes

**Ingredients:**
- 500g fresh seasoned sausage patties
- Olive oil spray
- 12 mini buns, sliced
- 60g mustard
- 60g ketchup

**Preparation Instructions:**
1. Preheat the air fryer to 180°C for 3 minutes.
2. Place the sausage patties in the drawers of the dual-zone air fryer.
3. Set zone 1 to 'AIR FRY' at 180°C for 5 minutes and zone 2 to 'ROAST' at 160°C for 3 minutes.
4. Press 'SYNC' and then 'STOP/START' to begin cooking.
5. Flip the sausage patties halfway through the cooking process.
6. Once cooked, assemble the patties in the mini buns with mustard and ketchup.
7. Secure each slider with a toothpick and serve.

# Potato Pancakes with Spicy Dip

Serves: 4 / Prep time: 35 minutes / Cook Time: 25 minutes

**Ingredients:**
- 600g potatoes, grated
- One small leek, chopped
- One large egg, beaten
- 20g oat flour
- 1 tsp paprika
- 1 tbsp olive oil
- Sea salt and black pepper, to taste
- Spicy Sauce:
- 100ml tomato sauce
- 50ml mayonnaise
- 1 chilli pepper, deseeded and finely chopped
- 1 tsp cayenne pepper

**Instructions:**
1. Place crisper plates in both drawers and spray with nonstick cooking oil.
2. Grate the potatoes and place them in a bowl of cold water for 30 minutes.
3. Drain the potatoes and mix them with the remaining Ingredients. Shape the mixture into small patties and arrange them in both drawers.
4. Set zone 1 to "AIR FRY" at 185°C for 25 minutes. Press "MATCH" and then the "START/STOP" button.
5. At the 8-minute mark, flip the potato cakes and resume cooking.
6. Meanwhile, mix all the Ingredients for the spicy sauce. Serve the potato cakes with the sauce on the side.

# Sticky Spicy Meatballs

Serves: 6 / Prep time: 10 minutes / Cook Time: 20 minutes

### Ingredients:
- Meatballs:
- 400g low-fat sausage
- 100g porridge oats
- 80g grated Parmesan cheese
- Two spring onions, chopped
- Two garlic cloves, minced
- A small handful of chopped parsley
- Sauce:
- 2 tbsp soy sauce
- 1 tbsp maple syrup
- Sea salt and black pepper, to taste
- 1 tbsp olive oil

### Instructions:
1. In a large bowl, combine all the meatball Ingredients and form the mixture into balls.
2. Set zone 1 to "AIR FRY" at 185°C for 20 minutes. Press "MATCH" to duplicate the settings for both zones and start the cooking process.
3. While the meatballs cook, mix all the sauce Ingredients.
4. At the halfway mark, turn the meatballs over and drizzle them with the sauce before resuming cooking.
5. Serve the meatballs with toothpicks.

# Brussels Sprouts with Soy-Maple Glaze

Serves: 6 / Prep time: 10 minutes / Cook Time: 13 minutes

### Ingredients:
- 800g Brussels sprouts
- 2 tbsp corn flour
- 2 tbsp melted butter
- 2 tbsp soy sauce
- 2 tbsp maple syrup
- Sea salt and black pepper, to taste

### Instructions:
1. Place the Brussels sprouts in two roasting tins and toss with the other Ingredients.
2. Set zone 1 to "ROAST" at 190°C for 13 minutes. Press "MATCH" to duplicate settings across both zones, then press "START/STOP."
3. At the halfway point, shake the baskets and continue cooking.

# Falafel with Vegetables

Serves: 5 / Prep time: 10 minutes / Cook Time: 20 minutes

### Ingredients:
- 400g canned chickpeas, drained and rinsed
- One large courgette, peeled
- One large carrot, peeled
- One small leek
- Two garlic cloves, peeled
- One medium bell pepper, deseeded
- One chilli pepper, deseeded
- 4 tbsp tomato puree

### Instructions:
1. Insert the crisper plates in both drawers and spray with cooking oil.
2. Blend all the Ingredients in a food processor until smooth. Shape the mixture into 10 balls and place them in the drawers.
3. Set zone 1 to "AIR FRY" at 185°C for 20 minutes. Press "MATCH" to duplicate the settings across both zones and start cooking.
4. After 10 minutes, turn the falafel balls over and continue cooking.
5. Serve the warm falafel with toothpicks.

# Maple-Glazed Crispy Wings

Serves: 4 / Prep time: 10 minutes / Cook Time: 33 minutes

### Ingredients:
- 800g chicken wings (drumettes and flats)
- 1 tbsp sesame oil
- 1 tbsp corn flour
- 1 tsp red pepper flakes
- 1 tsp garlic granules
- Sea salt and black pepper, to taste
- 2 tbsp Worcestershire sauce
- 2 tbsp maple syrup

### Instructions:
1. Place crisper plates in both drawers and spray with nonstick cooking oil.
2. Toss the chicken wings with the remaining Ingredients and divide them between the drawers.
3. Set zone 1 to "AIR FRY" at 200°C for 33 minutes. Press "MATCH" and then "START/STOP" to cook.
4. Cook until the wings are slightly charred on top. Enjoy!

# Hummus with Veggie Chips

Serves: 4 / Prep time: 10 minutes / Cook Time: 3 minutes

## Ingredients:
- 240g canned chickpeas, rinsed and drained
- Two garlic cloves
- 2 tbsp tahini
- 2 tbsp lemon juice
- 2 tbsp extra virgin olive oil
- 1/2 tsp ground cumin
- Salt and black pepper, to taste
- Assorted vegetable crisps for serving

## Instructions:
1. In a food processor, blend the chickpeas, garlic, tahini, lemon juice, olive oil, cumin, salt, and pepper until smooth.
2. Scrape down the sides as needed and adjust the seasoning to taste.
3. Air fry at 175°C for 3 minutes.
4. Transfer the hummus to a serving dish.
5. Serve with assorted vegetable crisps like carrot sticks, cucumber slices, pepper strips, or celery sticks.

# Classic Pesto Sauce

Makes: About 180ml / Prep time: 10 minutes / Cook Time: 3-4 minutes

## Ingredients:
- 50g fresh basil leaves
- 30g pine nuts
- 30g grated Parmesan cheese
- Two garlic cloves
- 120ml extra virgin olive oil
- Salt and black pepper, to taste

## Instructions:
1. In a food processor or blender, combine basil, pine nuts, Parmesan, and garlic.
2. Pulse a few times to break down the Ingredients.
3. With the processor running, gradually add the olive oil until the pesto is smooth.
4. Taste and season with salt and black pepper as needed.
5. Air fry at 180°C for 3-4 minutes.
6. Transfer the pesto to a jar with a tight lid.
7. Store in the refrigerator for up to one week.

## Sun-Dried Tomato Tapenade

Serves: 4 / Prep time: 10 minutes / Cook Time: 5 minutes

**Ingredients:**
- 240g sun-dried tomatoes in oil
- 60g pitted kalamata olives
- 60g fresh basil leaves
- Two garlic cloves, peeled
- 2 tbsp capers
- 2 tbsp olive oil
- 2 tbsp fresh lemon juice
- Salt and black pepper, to taste

**Instructions:**
1. Drain the sun-dried tomatoes from their oil and give them a rough chop.
2. In a food processor, combine the sun-dried tomatoes, kalamata olives, basil leaves, garlic, capers, olive oil, and lemon juice. Pulse until you achieve a coarse paste.
3. Season the mixture with salt and black pepper to your liking.
4. Place the tapenade in the air fryer basket and cook at 160°C for 5 minutes.
5. Serve the tapenade with bread, crackers, or vegetable sticks.

## Refried Bean Dip

Serves: 4-6 / Prep time: 10 minutes / Cook Time: 10 minutes

**Ingredients:**
- 400g canned pinto beans, drained and rinsed
- 1 tbsp olive oil
- One small onion, diced
- One garlic clove, minced
- 1/2 tsp ground cumin
- 1/4 tsp chilli powder
- Salt, to taste
- 60ml water
- Fresh cilantro, chopped (optional, for garnish)

**Instructions:**
1. Heat the olive oil in a saucepan over medium heat.
2. Add the diced onion and minced garlic, sautéing until the onion becomes translucent.
3. Stir in the ground cumin and chilli powder, cooking for an extra minute to enhance the flavour of the spices.
4. Add the pinto beans, season with salt, and pour in the water. Bring the mixture to a simmer.
5. Lower the heat and let the beans simmer for about 5 minutes to allow the flavours to blend.
6. Mash the beans to your desired consistency using a potato masher or fork.
7. If the dip is too thick, add a bit more water and continue mashing until smooth.
8. Taste and adjust the seasoning if needed.
9. Remove from heat, transfer to a serving bowl, and garnish with fresh chopped cilantro if desired.
10. Serve warm with tortilla chips or use as a filling for quesadillas and burritos.

# 7
# Snacks and Desserts

# Banana Cupcakes

Serves: 8 / Prep time: 10 minutes / Cook Time: 20 minutes

**Ingredients:**
- Two bananas, mashed
- 1 tsp ground cinnamon
- A pinch of grated nutmeg
- A pinch of salt
- 50g coconut oil at room temperature
- 100g golden caster sugar
- 150g oat flour
- 1 tsp baking powder
- 50g dried currants
- Buttercream, for decoration

**Instructions:**
1. In a bowl, mix all the dry Ingredients together. In another bowl, blend the liquid Ingredients. Combine the liquid mixture with the dry Ingredients and stir well.
2. Gently fold in the currants. Spoon the batter into lightly greased muffin cases.
3. Set the air fryer to 180°C and cook in zone 1 for 20 minutes. Press "MATCH" and then "START/STOP."
4. Allow the cupcakes to cool completely before removing them from their cases. Decorate with buttercream and enjoy!

# Easy Almond Fudge

Serves: 10 / Prep time: 12 minutes / Cook Time: 18 minutes

**Ingredients:**
- Cake:
- 200g dark chocolate (70-85% cacao), chopped
- 150g unsalted butter at room temperature
- 40g cocoa powder
- One large egg
- 180g brown sugar
- 60g oat flour
- 1/2 tsp ground cloves
- 1/2 tsp ground cinnamon
- 60g chopped almonds
- Topping:
- 200ml condensed milk
- 150g smooth almond butter
- 150g dark chocolate (70-85% cacao), chopped

**Instructions:**
1. Butter two baking tins and set aside.
2. Melt the chocolate, butter, and cocoa powder in the microwave, whisking until smooth.
3. Beat the egg with brown sugar until frothy, then add the remaining cake Ingredients and mix. Fold in the melted chocolate mixture.
4. Set zone 1 to "BAKE" at 180°C for 18 minutes. Press "MATCH" and then "START/STOP."
5. Meanwhile, melt the topping Ingredients in a heatproof bowl over simmering water.
6. Spread the topping over the cooled fudge base. Enjoy!

# Mini Cherry Bakewell Tarts

Serves: 4 / Prep time: 20 minutes / Cook Time: 10 minutes

### Ingredients:
- One sheet ready-rolled puff pastry (approx. 320g)
- 100g cherry jam
- 50g ground almonds
- 50g icing sugar
- 1/2 tsp almond extract
- 60ml water
- Flaked almonds for garnish (optional)

### Instructions:
1. Preheat the other zone of the air fryer to 180°C for 5 minutes.
2. Cut the puff pastry into squares and press them into the silicone muffin cups in the air fryer basket.
3. In a bowl, combine cherry jam, ground almonds, icing sugar, almond extract, and water.
4. Spoon the cherry almond mixture into each puff pastry cup.
5. Garnish with flaked almonds if desired.
6. Place the muffin cups in the air fryer basket.
7. Air fry at 180°C for 10 minutes or until the pastry is golden brown.
8. Allow to cool slightly before serving.

# Classic Brownie

Serves: 10 / Prep time: 12 minutes / Cook Time: 20 minutes

### Ingredients:
- 200g dark chocolate (70-85% cacao), chopped
- 150g unsalted butter at room temperature
- 150g brown sugar
- Two large eggs, lightly beaten
- 200g oat flour
- 1 tsp ground cinnamon
- 1 tsp vanilla paste
- 1/2 tsp ground cloves

### Instructions:
1. Grease two baking tins with cooking oil.
2. Melt the chocolate, butter, and sugar together in the microwave or a saucepan over low heat, stirring until smooth.
3. Mix in the eggs, then stir in the remaining Ingredients until well combined.
4. Set zone 1 to "BAKE" at 170°C for 20 minutes. Press "MATCH" and then "START/STOP."
5. Let the brownies cool on a rack for about 10 minutes before cutting and serving. Enjoy!

# Cinnamon Sugar Apple Chips

Serves: 4 / Prep time: 10 minutes / Cook Time: 2 hours

**Ingredients:**
- Four medium apples, thinly sliced
- 1 tbsp lemon juice
- 1 tsp ground cinnamon
- 2 tbsp granulated sugar

**Instructions:**
1. Preheat one zone of the air fryer to 70°C for 5 minutes.
2. Toss the apple slices in lemon juice to prevent browning.
3. Mix the cinnamon and granulated sugar together in a bowl.
4. Sprinkle the cinnamon sugar mixture over the apple slices and toss to coat evenly.
5. Arrange the apple slices in the air fryer basket without overlapping.
6. Air fry at 70°C for 2 hours, flipping the slices halfway through.
7. Once crisp and golden, remove from the air fryer and let cool before serving.

# Cinnamon Apple Fritters

Serves: 5 / Prep time: 5 minutes / Cook Time: 18 minutes

**Ingredients:**
- 200g self-raising flour
- 1/2 tsp baking powder
- 1/2 tsp vanilla extract
- 1 tsp ground cinnamon
- A pinch of ground cloves
- A pinch of sea salt
- Two eggs
- 60g brown sugar
- 100ml full-fat milk
- Two medium apples, cored and grated
- 2 tbsp vegetable oil

**Instructions:**
1. Line both drawers with parchment paper.
2. Mix the dry Ingredients in a bowl.
3. Separate the egg yolks from the whites. Beat the yolks with brown sugar and milk. Whip the egg whites until stiff peaks form.
4. Gently fold the egg whites into the yolk mixture.
5. Combine the wet and dry Ingredients, then fold in the grated apples.
6. Use a cookie scoop to drop batter onto the parchment-lined drawers. Drizzle with vegetable oil.
7. Set zone 1 to "AIR FRY" at 180°C for 18 minutes. Press "MATCH" and then "START/STOP."

## Twisted Halloumi Pigs in Blankets

Serves: 6 / Prep time: 10 minutes / Cook Time: 15 minutes

**Ingredients:**
- Five rashers pancetta, halved lengthwise
- Ten pieces halloumi (20g each), casing removed
- 1 tsp English mustard powder
- 1 tsp hot paprika

**Instructions:**
1. Place crisper plates in both drawers and spray with non-stick cooking oil.
2. Wrap halloumi pieces in pancetta slices and arrange them in the drawers. Sprinkle it with mustard powder and paprika.
3. Set zone 1 to "AIR FRY" at 180°C for 15 minutes. Press "MATCH" and then "START/STOP."
4. Turn the pieces halfway through cooking. Enjoy!

## Peanut Butter Cookies

Serves: 8 / Prep time: 15 minutes / Cook Time: 15 minutes

**Ingredients:**
- 100g plain flour
- 100g oat flour
- 1 tsp baking powder
- 120g honey
- 100g peanut butter at room temperature
- 1/2 tsp ground cinnamon
- 1 tsp vanilla extract
- 120ml almond milk
- 50g raisins

**Instructions:**
1. Preheat the Air Fryer to 180°C for 5 minutes.
2. Combine the dry Ingredients in a bowl until it resembles breadcrumbs.
3. In another bowl, mix the wet Ingredients thoroughly. Combine with the dry mixture, fold in the raisins, and stir well.
4. Use an ice cream scoop to shape the dough into balls and place them on parchment-lined baking tins.
5. Set zone 1 to "BAKE" at 180°C for 15 minutes. Press "MATCH" and then "START/STOP."
6. Allow cookies to cool for about 10 minutes before serving. Enjoy!

# Mini Autumn Pies

Serves: 8 / Prep time: 12 minutes / Cook Time: 14 minutes

### Ingredients:
- Two large apples, peeled, cored, and diced
- 60g brown sugar
- 1 tsp ground cinnamon
- 1/2 tsp freshly grated nutmeg
- 2 tbsp cornstarch
- Eight spring roll wrappers
- 2 tbsp melted coconut oil

### Instructions:
1. Combine the apples, brown sugar, cinnamon, nutmeg, and cornstarch in a mixing bowl.
2. Lay the spring roll wrappers on a flat surface. Distribute the apple mixture evenly among the wrappers.
3. Fold the wrappers diagonally to form triangles, seal the edges, and brush with melted coconut oil.
4. Line two baking tins with parchment paper.
5. Set zone 1 to "BAKE" at 175°C for 14 minutes. Press "MATCH" and then "START/STOP."
6. Enjoy your mini pies!

# Classic Mug Cake

Serves: 4 / Prep time: 10 minutes / Cook Time: 10 minutes

### Ingredients:
- Two large bananas, peeled and mashed
- Four medium eggs
- 2 tbsp coconut oil
- A pinch of ground cinnamon
- 1 tsp vanilla extract
- 100ml Mediterranean honey
- 50g oat flour
- 1 tsp baking powder
- 50g chocolate chips

### Instructions:
1. Beat the eggs until they are pale and frothy, then add the other Ingredients and mix well.
2. Divide the mixture among four ramekins. Place the ramekins into both drawers.
3. Set zone 1 to "BAKE" at 180°C for 10 minutes. Press "MATCH" and then "START/STOP."
4. Enjoy your mug cakes!

# Mini Sticky Toffee Puddings

Serves: 4 / Prep time: 5 minutes / Cook Time: 10 minutes

### Ingredients:
- Four large chocolate chip muffins
- 50g large raisins
- 1-cal butter spray
- For the Sauce:
- 25g light muscovado sugar
- 25g dark muscovado sugar
- 50g butter
- 75ml heavy cream
- 200g vanilla ice cream

### Instructions:
1. Crumble the muffins and mix with raisins.
2. Place the mixture into four greased mini-baking pots.
3. Cover the pots with foil and place two pots in each zone of the air fryer.
4. Set the zones to "BAKE" at 200°C for 9 minutes. Press "MATCH" and then "START/STOP."
5. Meanwhile, combine the muscovado sugars, butter, and cream in a pan and heat until the sugar dissolves and the sauce thickens.
6. Pour the toffee sauce over the muffin mixture. Top each pot with 50g of vanilla ice cream.

# The Best Crème Brûlée Ever

Serves: 4 / Prep time: 10 minutes / Cook Time: 22 minutes

### Ingredients:
- 250ml heavy cream
- 1 tsp vanilla essence
- 200ml milk
- Three large eggs
- 200g granulated sugar
- Garnish:
- 2 tbsp brown sugar
- 4 tbsp berries of your choice

### Instructions:
1. In a saucepan, combine cream, vanilla, milk, and eggs, whisking until well mixed.
2. Stir in the granulated sugar and cook until the sugar dissolves. Remove from heat and pour the mixture into ramekins.
3. Place the ramekins into both drawers of the air fryer.
4. Set zone 1 to "BAKE" at 190°C for 20 minutes. Press "MATCH" and then "START/STOP."
5. Before serving, sprinkle brown sugar and berries on top. Caramelise the sugar under 200°C for 2 minutes.

# Chinese Spring Rolls With Sweet Chilli Sauce

Serves: 16 / Prep time: 40 minutes / Cook Time: 12 minutes

**Ingredients:**
- 16 spring roll wrappers
- 1 tbsp sesame oil
- One garlic clove, minced
- 300g carrots, chopped into thin sticks
- 200g mushrooms
- 1 tbsp fish sauce
- 1 tbsp cornstarch
- To Serve:
- 250ml sweet chilli sauce
- Two medium eggs
- 1-cal olive oil spray
- 350g diced cabbage
- 60ml lime juice
- 1 tbsp soy sauce

**Instructions:**
1. Preheat the air fryer to 200°C for 6 minutes.
2. Heat sesame oil in a large pan over medium heat, then add the minced garlic.
3. Add the vegetables to the pan and cook until tender.
4. Remove from heat and stir in the fish sauce, soy sauce, and lime juice.
5. Fill each spring roll wrapper with the vegetable mixture, fold tightly, and seal the edges.
6. In a bowl, mix the egg with cornstarch to form a paste. Brush this paste onto the spring rolls.
7. Place eight spring rolls in each zone of the air fryer and spray with olive oil.
8. Set both zones to "AIR FRY" at 200°C for 6 minutes. Press "MATCH" and then "START/STOP."
9. Flip the spring rolls halfway through cooking. Serve with sweet chilli sauce.

# 8
# Family Favourites

# Traditional Steak and Kidney Pie

Serves: 8-10 / Prep time: 5 minutes / Cook time: 15 minutes

## Ingredients:
- 1 kg steak and kidney filling
- Four sheets puff pastry
- Olive oil spray
- Two eggs, beaten

## Instructions:
1. Preheat the Ninja Dual Zone Air Fryer to 180°C for 6 minutes.
2. While the air fryer preheats, cut out four pastry sheets to fit 6-inch baking tins.
3. Thoroughly spray two 6-inch baking tins with olive oil spray.
4. Line each tin with a layer of pastry, add the steak and kidney filling, and cover with another layer of pastry.
5. Make a small incision in the centre of each pie to allow steam to escape.
6. Brush the tops of the pies with beaten eggs.
7. Place one pie in each drawer of the air fryer. Set both zones to "BAKE" at 180°C and cook for 12-15 minutes until the pastry is golden and puffed.
8. Once done, slice each pie into 4-5 portions and serve hot. Enjoy!

# Sweet & Sour Chicken Balls

Serves: 2 / Prep time: 6 minutes / Cook time: 12 minutes

## Ingredients:
- Frozen chicken balls
- Frozen sweet & sour sauce
- 1 tsp extra virgin olive oil

## Instructions:
1. Preheat the Ninja Dual Zone Air Fryer to 180°C.
2. Place the frozen chicken balls in the air fryer basket.
3. Cook for 8 minutes at 180°C. During this time, add the frozen sweet & sour sauce sachet to the air fryer to heat it up.
4. After 8 minutes, shake the basket, spray the chicken balls lightly with olive oil, and increase the temperature to 200°C.
5. Cook for an additional 4 minutes or until the chicken balls are crispy and golden.
6. Serve the chicken balls hot with the warmed sweet & sour sauce on the side. Enjoy!

# Sweet Potato Fries with Cinnamon Sugar and Nutmeg

Serves: 2 / Prep time: 10 minutes / Cook time: 22 minutes

## Ingredients:
- 450g sweet potatoes, peeled and cut into thin fries
- 1 tbsp olive oil
- 1 tsp ground cinnamon
- 1/2 tsp ground nutmeg
- 2 tbsp granulated sugar
- Salt and black pepper, to taste

## Instructions:
1. Preheat the Ninja Dual Zone Air Fryer to 200°C.
2. In a large bowl, toss the sweet potato fries with olive oil, then season with salt and black pepper.
3. Place the sweet potato fries in zone 1 of the air fryer and set it to "AIR FRY" at 200°C for 12 minutes.
4. While the fries cook, mix together the cinnamon, nutmeg, and sugar in a separate bowl.
5. After 12 minutes, transfer the fries to zone 2 and continue cooking on "AIR FRY" for another 10 minutes or until they are crispy.
6. Immediately after cooking, toss the hot sweet potato fries in the cinnamon sugar mixture. Serve right away and enjoy!

# References

- 50 *air fryer recipes for beginners*. (2022, June 24). Www.taste.com.au. https://www.taste.com.au/galleries/air-fryer-recipes-beginners/sogybuzd
- *Air Fryer Recipes*. (n.d.-a). Allrecipes. https://www.allrecipes.com/recipes/23070/everyday-cooking/cookware-and-equipment/air-fryer/
- *Air fryer recipes*. (n.d.-b). BBC Good Food. https://www.bbcgoodfood.com/recipes/collection/air-fryer-recipes
- *Air Fryer Recipes | Food Network UK*. (n.d.). Foodnetwork.co.uk. https://foodnetwork.co.uk/collections/air-fryer-recipes
- *Air Fryer Recipes Archives*. (2021). Ministry of Curry. https://ministryofcurry.com/recipes/airfryer-recipes/
- *Air fryer Recipes Archives*. (2023). Confessions of a Fit Foodie. https://confessionsofafitfoodie.com/category/recipes/cooking-method/airfryer/
- airfryeraddicts. (2022, April 2). Air Fryer Addicts. Air Fryer Addicts. https://airfryeraddicts.com/
- Cooks, P. (2024). *Airfryer Recipes | Poppy Cooks*. Poppy Cooks. https://www.poppycooks.com/series/air-fryer/
- https://www.facebook.com/seriouseats. (2024). *18 Air Fryer Recipes Our Editors Love for Easy, Speedy Meals*. Serious Eats. https://www.seriouseats.com/best-air-fryer-recipes-8681529
- JamieOliver.com. (n.d.). *Air-fryer recipes | Jamie Oliver*. Jamie Oliver. https://www.jamieoliver.com/recipes/air-fryer-recipes/
- *Salter Air Fryer Recipes*. (2024). Salter.com. https://salter.com/air-fryer-recipes
- Szewczyk, J. (2018, November 16). *15 of Our Favorite Air Fryer Recipes to Make Immediately*. Kitchn; Apartment Therapy, LLC. https://www.thekitchn.com/air-fryer-recipes-264238
- *The Best Air Fryer Recipes - Healthy & Easy!* (2023). Skinnytaste. https://www.skinnytaste.com/recipes/air-fryer/
- Villarosa, D. (2022, January 21). *You Won't Believe Everything You Can Make in an Air Fryer*. Delish. https://www.delish.com/cooking/g4711/air-fryer-recipes/

# Image References

- https://www.pexels.com/photo/brown-bread-on-gray-textile-10687590/
- https://unsplash.com/photos/brown-sausage-on-stainless-steel-tray-Y8C91gKAmLo
- https://unsplash.com/photos/sliced-avocado-on-white-ceramic-plate-npy4g1JTuoM
- https://unsplash.com/photos/a-plate-of-food-3l0MDo_qdjQ
- https://unsplash.com/photos/sliced-pie-on-wooden-board-lBlwuzreCtI
- https://unsplash.com/photos/a-couple-of-pans-filled-with-potatoes-on-top-of-a-tiled-floor-jRKM2fmDXyM
- https://unsplash.com/photos/a-plate-of-crab-cakes-with-lemon-wedges-pickles-and-pickles-fCL8jnVtDr8
- https://unsplash.com/photos/chocolate-ice-cream-in-white-ceramic-bowl-s_f1RqDVDDo
- https://unsplash.com/photos/brown-and-white-round-cookies-on-white-ceramic-plate-Dy0n61YrhxM
- https://unsplash.com/photos/a-plate-of-food-_Tci2omfmHI
- https://unsplash.com/photos/a-white-bowl-filled-with-yellow-liquid-on-top-of-a-wooden-table-0RlzOssfQ5Y
- https://unsplash.com/photos/a-bowl-of-ice-cream-mXQh9lLzTYo
- https://unsplash.com/photos/three-pans-filled-with-scrambled-eggs-and-toast-GsuOv5FFVf0
- https://unsplash.com/photos/burger-on-white-ceramic-plate-dFubWB-pnik
- https://unsplash.com/photos/a-white-plate-topped-with-crackers-and-eggs-jzEFuLeMu6E
- https://unsplash.com/photos/a-plate-of-food-and-a-drink-on-a-table-rjgv_Tqoe3c
- https://unsplash.com/photos/a-table-topped-with-tacos-covered-in-sauce-and-toppings-rHtP-U7bN4I
- https://unsplash.com/photos/a-wooden-cutting-board-topped-with-fried-chicken-wings-HKMuI0gjlPc
- https://unsplash.com/photos/a-loaf-of-bread-sitting-on-top-of-a-cutting-board-R1CQAw0mqcA
- https://unsplash.com/photos/a-bowl-of-salad-on-a-wooden-table-Pfcc44P32vQ
- https://unsplash.com/photos/a-plate-of-chicken-wings-with-a-dipping-sauce-HXvDcfwbHiY
- https://unsplash.com/photos/a-bowl-of-beans-and-bread-on-a-table-l1FippuRBFE
- https://unsplash.com/photos/cooked-food-on-white-ceramic-plate-Y-CSSwcS5co
- https://unsplash.com/photos/a-close-up-view-of-a-carpet-texture-0zgiwzaE5fo
- https://unsplash.com/photos/a-burrito-cut-in-half-on-a-plate-next-to-a-bottle-of-beer-ah2fCJP9Eok
- https://unsplash.com/photos/a-glass-bowl-filled-with-meat-and-vegetables--bOq74RhBec
- https://unsplash.com/photos/a-close-up-of-a-steak-on-a-plate-cdyZGJNax3Y
- https://unsplash.com/photos/a-pan-filled-with-food-sitting-on-top-of-a-table-H-D-0UOgzMc
- https://unsplash.com/photos/a-black-bowl-filled-with-green-beans-next-to-a-camera-uybcBKbBFvY
- https://unsplash.com/photos/roti-and-meat-slices-with-sauce-on-plate-ZSukCSw5VV4
- https://unsplash.com/photos/yellow-corn-on-glass-bowl-h83Rm3njjcg
- https://unsplash.com/photos/cooked-food-on-blue-ceramic-plate-BKSntHf8oiU

- https://unsplash.com/photos/two-raw-fish-fillets-sit-on-a-cutting-board-TPaDFQwDaj4
- https://unsplash.com/photos/a-white-plate-topped-with-scallops-and-vegetables-ShKo5FF8Ljk
- https://unsplash.com/photos/a-plate-of-food-7WBbsJqhTtQ
- https://unsplash.com/photos/two-fish-hanging-from-hooks-on-a-fence--YKznhQ_IVw
- https://unsplash.com/photos/a-sandwich-with-lettuce-tomato-and-onion-on-a-wooden-board-kxDJNdZpkc4
- https://unsplash.com/photos/a-person-sitting-at-a-table-with-a-plate-of-food-Bilacmu3P_c
- https://unsplash.com/photos/a-close-up-of-a-plate-of-food-on-a-table-kEYieb7pzAM
- https://unsplash.com/photos/cooked-food-on-brown-wooden-bowl-JocD18QpAkY
- https://unsplash.com/photos/fish-covered-with-white-white-pasee-ddjPCuHwN50
- https://unsplash.com/photos/a-blue-plate-topped-with-sliced-tomatoes-and-a-fork-U1w5IDSOVeg
- https://unsplash.com/photos/a-plastic-container-filled-with-lots-of-shrimp-cAGB3DoWIm8
- https://unsplash.com/photos/cooked-food-on-black-ceramic-bowl-HNmcgpzPHag
- https://unsplash.com/photos/fish-dish-with-sliced-lemon-zOYuGvDlZ7g
- https://unsplash.com/photos/a-couple-of-raw-meat-on-a-cutting-board-VpSwmt0-FMQ
- https://unsplash.com/photos/roasted-meat-served-on-ceramic-plate-Hs5gvdM8qo8
- https://unsplash.com/photos/raw-meat-on-stainless-steel-tray-MEnlQv-EQvY
- https://unsplash.com/photos/a-white-plate-topped-with-meat-and-veggies-wkms_RlOuDU
- https://unsplash.com/photos/cooked-food-on-white-ceramic-plate-70e-y6eFqQs
- https://unsplash.com/photos/a-person-in-a-chefs-coat-is-making-food-D5PigOkXNKg
- https://unsplash.com/photos/a-plate-of-food-on-a-marble-table-VxfciD23qpY
- https://unsplash.com/photos/brown-and-black-bread-on-white-table-41IXII03_A0
- https://unsplash.com/photos/sliced-meat-on-white-ceramic-plate-XRcwELmjLgs
- https://unsplash.com/photos/woman-in-white-tank-top-holding-spoon-with-rice-zAjP6XUrqeQ
- https://unsplash.com/photos/a-man-cutting-up-a-piece-of-meat-on-a-cutting-board-ILGu7fO8-RA
- https://unsplash.com/photos/a-man-standing-in-front-of-a-table-full-of-food-S8vwarzaqSo
- https://unsplash.com/photos/a-white-plate-topped-with-a-salad-and-a-fork-DIcMloz85KY
- https://unsplash.com/photos/cooked-dish-HMbjq6BucM8
- https://unsplash.com/photos/brown-burger-dish-on-white-ceramic-plate-4hgYULBzVEE
- https://unsplash.com/photos/a-piece-of-food-on-a-wooden-surface-fsQPy6AtSYM
- https://unsplash.com/photos/brown-chopping-board-1xGKxpCoM5s
- https://unsplash.com/photos/white-and-brown-floral-textile-r5oZ-DJ2E8I
- https://unsplash.com/photos/yellow-and-white-sliced-fruit-on-brown-wooden-table-1nO6i8BkC1g
- https://unsplash.com/photos/bowlful-of-vegetable-salad-RCyXyaim87Y
- https://unsplash.com/photos/green-vegetables-on-top-of-white-board-la6DtkODelg
- https://unsplash.com/photos/a-tray-of-cut-up-vegetables-on-a-table-ZWKLCjeAdZ8
- https://unsplash.com/photos/a-white-plate-topped-with-meatballs-and-a-salad-WVoLfiKbYBQ

- https://unsplash.com/photos/slice-squash-lot-ubkJke6IJ3I
- https://unsplash.com/photos/a-bowl-of-chickpeas-on-a-white-table-Y3P44nmBobE
- https://unsplash.com/photos/a-black-plate-with-a-mushroom-inside-of-it-cBOGycu-s_Y
- https://unsplash.com/photos/text-1qiifK3y8FE
- https://unsplash.com/photos/broccoli-vegetable-UrqPUe3zUzw
- https://unsplash.com/photos/ladies-finger-lo-uDeMugA9ojU
- https://unsplash.com/photos/a-person-holding-a-bowl-of-fried-food-fJc41-CtN_0
- https://unsplash.com/photos/brown-mushrooms-on-gray-surface-XJY1C5LVNn8
- https://unsplash.com/photos/orange-fruits-on-stainless-steel-tray-jgTZN6sDrGU
- https://unsplash.com/photos/vegetable-salad-on-white-ceramic-bowl-EvoIiaIVRzU
- https://unsplash.com/photos/six-cupcakes-on-red-round-plate-ZHCn1GBpczc
- https://unsplash.com/photos/crutons-and-salad-dish-gNfZVRZOdlY
- https://unsplash.com/photos/a-person-holding-a-cut-in-half-sandwich-gaZAPg6Tol8
- https://unsplash.com/photos/person-holding-a-plate-with-bread-cLnuyhnuaTc
- https://unsplash.com/photos/a-person-holding-a-tray-of-doughnuts-on-a-sidewalk-LmHK7VeCwZ4
- https://unsplash.com/photos/savory-chicken-on-plate-Yh9Ut4d3K0A
- https://unsplash.com/photos/a-table-topped-with-plates-of-food-and-a-bowl-of-dip-YyZoVGbwkfA
- https://unsplash.com/photos/a-close-up-of-a-bunch-of-green-flowers-iWrb1ytjvNQ
- https://unsplash.com/photos/white-ceramic-bowl-with-soup-FBbGyco88GU
- https://unsplash.com/photos/vegetable-grind-in-mortar-and-pestle-2lEoPVy3oJ0
- https://unsplash.com/photos/closeup-photo-of-red-tomato-against-black-background-Sdc8PboZmI
- https://unsplash.com/photos/brown-coffee-beans-on-brown-wooden-surface-LBS8NZy6AOM
- https://unsplash.com/photos/cupcakes-on-white-ceramic-plate-QhIE94TpnkA
- https://unsplash.com/photos/a-bowl-of-chips-next-to-a-bowl-of-apples-31D8jOXzQQo
- https://unsplash.com/photos/sliced-cake-dish-UI6WBQOb2bM
- https://unsplash.com/photos/slice-of-brownies-beside-silver-strainers-yngPm-Jwc4I
- https://unsplash.com/photos/selective-focus-photo-of-gray-nut-ornament-zBIx3Ntc1kQ
- https://unsplash.com/photos/a-white-plate-topped-with-three-small-cakes-oCjU3isKl5U
- https://unsplash.com/photos/a-close-up-of-a-bowl-of-food-mEaaQU9MqHI
- https://unsplash.com/photos/person-holding-black-plastic-tray-U_SYUzDK4dA
- https://unsplash.com/photos/brown-and-white-pastry-on-brown-wooden-table-2oRH6vsVTC8
- https://unsplash.com/photos/two-white-ceramic-mug-with-chocolate-truffles-0nCXdttXbZA
- https://unsplash.com/photos/a-plate-of-food-5wWAIfnx1rM
- https://unsplash.com/photos/cooked-food-SiXUNNb6C80
- https://unsplash.com/photos/chocolate-cake-on-white-ceramic-plate-ZXmxQ0Ny_IY
- https://unsplash.com/photos/brown-pie-on-brown-wooden-table-HG1pJiQHXzs
- https://unsplash.com/photos/two-raw-chicken-breasts-in-a-black-bowl-9ZrWR8R961U
- https://unsplash.com/photos/cooked-food-with-wrapper-8tZ41RzaS7I

Printed in Great Britain
by Amazon